Editor-in-Chief and Founder:
  Lyndon H. LaRouche, Jr.
Editorial Board: *Lyndon H. LaRouche, Jr. , Helga Zepp-LaRouche, Robert Ingraham, Tony Papert, Gerald Rose, Dennis Small, Jeffrey Steinberg, William Wertz*
Co-Editors: *Robert Ingraham, Tony Papert*
Managing Editor: *Nancy Spannaus*
Technology: *Marsha Freeman*
Books: *Katherine Notley*
Ebooks: *Richard Burden*
Graphics: *Alan Yue*
Photos: *Stuart Lewis*
Circulation Manager: *Stanley Ezrol*

INTELLIGENCE DIRECTORS
Counterintelligence: *Jeffrey Steinberg, Michele Steinberg*
Economics: *John Hoefle, Marcia Merry Baker, Paul Gallagher*
History: *Anton Chaitkin*
Ibero-America: *Dennis Small*
Russia and Eastern Europe: *Rachel Douglas*
United States: *Debra Freeman*

INTERNATIONAL BUREAUS
Bogotá: *Miriam Redondo*
Berlin: *Rainer Apel*
Copenhagen: *Tom Gillesberg*
Houston: *Harley Schlanger*
Lima: *Sara Madueño*
Melbourne: *Robert Barwick*
Mexico City: *Gerardo Castilleja Chávez*
New Delhi: *Ramtanu Maitra*
Paris: *Christine Bierre*
Stockholm: *Ulf Sandmark*
United Nations, N.Y.C.: *Leni Rubinstein*
Washington, D.C.: *William Jones*
Wiesbaden: *Göran Haglund*

ON THE WEB
e-mail: eirns@larouchepub.com
www.larouchepub.com
www.executiveintelligencereview.com
www.larouchepub.com/eiw
Webmaster: *John Sigerson*
Assistant Webmaster: *George Hollis*
Editor, Arabic-language edition: *Hussein Askary*

EIR (ISSN 0273-6314) *is published weekly (50 issues), by EIR News Service, Inc., P.O. Box 17390, Washington, D.C. 20041-0390. (703) 777-9451 ext. 415*

European Headquarters: E.I.R. GmbH, Postfach Bahnstrasse 9a, D-65205, Wiesbaden, Germany Tel: 49-611-73650
Homepage: http://www.eirna.com
e-mail: eirna@eirna.com
Director: Georg Neudecker

Montreal, Canada: 514-461-1557
eir@eircanada.ca

Denmark: EIR - Danmark, Sankt Knuds Vej 11, basement left, DK-1903 Frederiksberg, Denmark. Tel.: +45 35 43 60 40, Fax: +45 35 43 87 57. e-mail: eirdk@hotmail.com.

Mexico City: EIR, Sor Juana Inés de la Cruz 242-2 Col. Agricultura C.P. 11360 Delegación M. Hidalgo, México D.F. Tel. (5525) 5318-2301
eirmexico@gmail.com

Copyright: ©2016 EIR News Service. All rights reserved. Reproduction in whole or in part without permission strictly prohibited.

Canada Post Publication Sales Agreement #40683579

Postmaster: Send all address changes to *EIR*, P.O. Box 17390, Washington, D.C. 20041-0390.

Signed articles in *EIR* represent the views of the authors, and not necessarily those of the Editorial Board.

What Is Science?

EIR Contents

www.larouchepub.com Volume 44, Number 12, March 24, 2017

Cover This Week

March 24, 2017 is the centenary of the birth of the great scientist Krafft A. Ehricke (left), who died in 1984. (To the right is Dr. Hans Rudolf Friedrich.)

General Dynamics Astronautics

WHAT IS SCIENCE?

I. What Is Science?

The Anthropology of Astronautics

by Krafft A. Ehricke

Astronautics, a publication of the American Rocket Society, originally published "The Anthropology of Astronautics" by Krafft A. Ehricke, in its November 1957 issue. Astronautics described Ehricke's article as "A searching examination by one of the leading thinkers in our field of the implications of space flight and its challenge to human destiny." Ehricke's article was later republished in a book, Krafft Ehricke's Extraterrestrial Imperative, *authored by Marsha Freeman, which was published by Apogee Books in 2008.*

From 1957: Krafft A. Ehricke is assistant to the Technical Director of the Astronautics Division of Convair in San Diego. After graduating as an aeronautical engineer in Berlin, Germany, he worked at Peenemünde on the V-2 project. In 1945 he obtained a contract from the Dept. of the Army. He worked from 1947 to 1950 as research engineer on ramjet and rocket systems at Ft. Bliss, Tex., and from 1950 to 1952 was at Redstone Arsenal, Ala., where he headed the Gasdynamics Section. From 1952 to 1954 he was with Bell Aircraft Corp. in Buffalo, N.Y., as preliminary design engineer. In 1954 he joined Convair, San Diego, as Design Specialist. Prior to his present position, he built up the Preliminary Design and Systems Analysis Group of the newly established Astronautics Div., and headed it for some time.

Altogether, in the United States and other countries, billions of dollars are now being spent on the development of a technology which gives every indication of being or becoming an astronautical technology. This is extremely gratifying to all those who, during the first part of this century, fought for recognition of space travel as a serious, practical and worthwhile effort—not at some future time, but right now, in this century and in this age of ours.

The campaign for technical and scientific recognition of space flight is won. However, the fight for recognition of astronautics as a vital part of man's future, rather than as just an accepted technical or scientific specialty, has hardly begun. Astronautics is the science of operating in space and traveling to other worlds. The implications are such that it now becomes increasingly important to develop the philosophy, as well as the utilitarian aspects, of this new science.

Since space travel has been recognized by its protagonists as one of the most fundamental and outstanding concepts in the history of man, it is not surprising that a good deal of thinking has already been done on this subject, beginning with Konstantin Ziolkowsky, whose ardent belief in the cosmic mission of mankind heralded the dawn of astronautic pioneering some 60 years ago, and continuing with Hermann Oberth, Willy Ley, A.C. Clarke, A.V. Cleaver, Wernher von Braun and Eugen Saenger. A certain mutual overlapping of thoughts and arguments advanced by these pioneers and others, is unavoidable, in view of the principal agreement among all concerned over the promotion of space travel.

However, the philosophy of astronautics is young and fertile. Its countless implications are far from exhausted. For this reason, the author, concerned for some 20 years with the study and the advocacy of astronautics as a technical, as well as a cultural, mission, submits a few additional thoughts on this subject.

The concept of space travel carries with it enormous impact, because it challenges man on practically all fronts of his physical and spiritual existence. The idea of traveling to other celestial bodies reflects to the highest degree the inde-

The Three Fundamental Laws Of Astronautics

First Law

Nobody and nothing under the natural laws of this universe impose any limitations on man except man himself.

Second Law

Not only the Earth, but the entire Solar system, and as much of the universe as he can reach under the laws of nature, are man's rightful field of activity.

Third Law

By expanding through the Universe, man fulfills his destiny as an element of life, endowed with the power of reason and the wisdom of the moral law within himself.

pendence and agility of the human mind. It lends ultimate dignity to man's technical and scientific endeavors. Above all, it touches on the philosophy of his very existence. As a result, the concept of space travel disregards national borders, refuses to recognize differences of historical or ethnological origin, and penetrates the fiber of one sociological or political creed as fast as that of the next.

As a technical concept, astronautics is all-embracing, and more revolutionary than anything conceived so far, including even atomic technology. As a scientific concept, it is bound to stimulate and rejuvenate practically all fields from astronomy to zoology. Its sociological and political implications are such that future generations may well describe as "cautious" even the boldest predictions of our time.

A Moving Spirit

Because of this, space travel holds perhaps the greatest general appeal for our complex and divided world. It seems to promise less immediate material gain than atomic technology. Yet, or perhaps therefore, its spiritual appeal is extremely powerful, symbolizing as it does that man, after all, has not yet lost his capability of cutting the Gordian knot, of exploding old notions which retard his development and of overcoming seemingly invincible physical obstacles.

If it can be done here, it can eventually also be done in other segments of our life today, where man seems to be hopelessly and perpetually deadlocked. A feeling of enthusiasm and genuine interest seems to prevail among all those who deal with space flight and astronautics—school children learning about it, Congressmen allotting money for it, political leaders of the East and West praising their nation's contributions to its progress, and last, but not least, scientists and engineers blazing the trail toward its eventual accomplishment.

Nevertheless, we must face the question: "Why space flight?" As an implication of a waste of time and money on a hopeless venture, this question is rarely asked today. Few people still doubt that we can, for instance, establish satellites which will serve useful purposes. As a request for philosophical justification of the vastly greater long-range implications of astronautics, an answer must be given, and given as firmly, conclusively and decisively as possible. It has already been recognized that a good deal of thinking is needed to provide this kind of answer, and we are just beginning to deal with the problem. We should not, however, let ourselves be stampeded into frantic attempts to "prove" a need for rushing to Venus or Mars, because, to put it bluntly, there really is none *today*.

Acceptance of Space Vehicle

The important point is to understand why we should gradually accept the space vehicle just as our ancestors finally got around to accepting the wheel and the boat. There was a time—the *Odyssey* proves it—when it was almost inconceivable for the ordinary man to leave his peninsula or island and sail beyond the horizon into the unknown. We still haven't changed much in principle, because it is still inconceivable for many of us to consider our Earth as an island from which one day many men may leave for distant places, unknown to us, except in a general way, or which one day may be visited by people from far away, as an American citizen today visits the country of his extraction.

As a contribution toward answering this famous question, I propose to establish a broad perspective by formulating three fundamental laws of astronautics [see box, this page], and examining their implications. These laws are the basic tenets in the pioneering of space flight, in the development of modern missile technology (as well as other technologies, notably the atomic), and in our ambitious plans and hopes regarding the future of astronautics.

The first law is astronautics' challenge to man to write his declaration of independence from *a priori* thinking, from uncritically accepted conditions, in other words, from a past and principally different pretechnological world clinging to him. This can be done. The Declaration of Independence and the Constitution of this country prove it. Implementation may take a long time, but the first breakthrough to its formulation is of decisive importance. These documents would probably never have been written in Europe, although the French Revolution is credited with stimulating much of the thought that went into them. A new world, mental distance emphasized by physical distance, and a fresh sociological start were necessary for their formulation.

Contains Many Variables

Europe and America (not only the United States), though related, are two separate differentiations of the integral of human civilizational capacity, like the Chinese, the Indian, the Roman, Hellenistic, Hebrew and many other civilizations before them. This integral contains innumerable variables, and the number of possible differentiations in time and space is therefore equally large, provided man's spirit is not snuffed out in the confinements of a too narrow cosmic environment.

Here we find an important trend: The gigantic scope of astronautics is doubtless one of the more immediate reasons for its fascinating challenge. It offers to take man where he has never been before, and therefore compellingly appeals to his inborn curiosity, love for adventure and dedication to research. However, beyond this, the most fundamental reason may be deeply hidden in a past so distant that it exceeds by far even the lifespan of his own species. A characteristic of life on this

NASA

"It is part of our heritage as children of this planet to seek out other worlds, to grow and to mature with our expanded capabilities into degrees of freedom and independence which would make present-day societies appear like the incredible confinements of medieval communities ..." During the Gemini 4 mission on June 3, 1965, Ed White became the first American to conduct a spacewalk.

planet, including man, is the desire to expand, to spread, to instinctively respond in an aggressive manner to the unknown, and to regard the seemingly unattainable as a provocation which must not remain unanswered.

The first great response of this type came with the expansion of life from the oceans to the land. Amphibia and reptiles reproduced the original conditions existing in the primeval oceans in their eggs, which were then hatched by the sun in a friendly, warm climate, the only climate in which they could exist. With a few exceptions, they remained crawling animals. Their bodies were in close contact with the ground, resulting in extensive heat exchange. Hence, their blood temperature followed, and today still follows, that of ground temperature. It cannot be kept at a constant moderate level like that of the mammals.

The development of the mammal, the most versatile

and perfect land animal, was a brilliant biotechnical achievement. Divorcing the body from the ground by means of legs freed the body from slavishly following the temperature cycle of the soil, permitted the development of insulating furs, and allowed the maintenance of a fairly constant temperature around 98°F, about the same as that of the primeval ocean waters. Now it was no longer necessary to lay eggs and depend on the sun for hatching. The brood could be developed in the motherbody itself. Therewith, life became almost independent of climatic conditions. The conquest of the land could be completed. Also, the lower atmosphere could be occupied in time by follow-on developments of the reptiles, which showed a better growth potential for this environment than mammals.

Found Itself Stymied

Then life found itself stymied on the borders of space. There are no biological means where direct application would permit living beings to enter, and cross space. It is intriguing to think that life may have answered this challenge by producing a new amphibian—man—whose restless mind reaches beyond the confinements of his biological world. The human brain alone is capable of utilizing certain superior qualities of inorganic matter for entering space.

And now begins the next act in the gigantic drama, with man holding a key role. Surrounded by protective shells, life sets out to spread to other worlds. Possibly it does so from several nuclei in space, many light years apart. In this perspective, it appears more difficult than not to assume that our response to the challenge of space flight should be limited to building earth satellites, unless we choose to impose this limit on ourselves. It is part of our heritage as children of this planet to seek out other worlds, to grow and to mature with our expanded capabilities into degrees of freedom and independence which would make present-day societies appear like the incredible confinements of medieval communities or African tribal regulations. It is a historical fact that man's mind and spirit grow with the space in which he is allowed to operate.

The importance of the second law can be measured by the effect which the expansion of European man all over the Earth had on the development of civilization. Medieval European civilization, frozen in the narrowness of its small, rigidly controlled communities and tightly bound to an all-powerful religious dogma, was

in the 12th and 13th Centuries dangerously close to becoming another static civilization, like those of ancient China, Japan, India or the Incas on this continent. Before it stretched a dreary succession of generations unchangingly channeled through a rigid, if not tyrannical, social and philosophical system for whose maintenance alone they were permitted to exist. The sudden recognition that here was the wide and beautiful Earth waiting to be taken by man, overwhelmed and emboldened the great thinkers of that time, notably Giordano Bruno, Nicolaus Copernicus, Galileo Galilei and Johannes Kepler. This was the crowning achievement of the Renaissance, and forever shattered the world of dogmatic scholasticism.

Now we begin to realize that the Solar system, and probably even part of this Galaxy, can be ours. The consequences, for all phases of human existence, of the practical application of the second law of astronautics during the coming centuries almost defies our imagination, just as the world of today would be almost inconceivable to the Renaissance pioneers. We today are merely the shipbuilders for the men and women who will enter a new era of discoveries and lay the foundations for those who will come after them, those who will develop planetary technologies and create cosmic civilizations.

The Third Law

The third law specifies this anthropological character of space operations as we humans can conceive it. It does not imply as desirable the brutal conquest of other worlds, such as happened frequently in the colonization of this world of ours. It does, however, proclaim man's natural right to explore and attempt to fertilize with human skill and wisdom all those parts of the universe which he can reach, whether or not they are inhabited by intelligent beings. This right is equally at the disposal of other civilizations in the universe if they can reach us first, or, if, in the course of their expansion, they reach other worlds before us.

The results of man's contact with another civilization in space, if and when this ever happens, can only be speculated upon. Of basic importance right now is the fact that man is the only source of intelligent life known to us, which gives him the right to expand, to develop and to enrich the foundations of his existence to the limits of his capability. In the light of this perspective, expeditions to other planets, i.e., the age of discovery, is

NASA

"Man's natural right to explore and attempt to fertilize with human skill and wisdom all those parts of the universe which he can reach..." Hubble Space Telescope view of Galaxy Messier 94.

We can also define the utility of a manned exploratory flight to Venus or Mars. Yet all these utilities are limited to special scientific or technical considerations, or to arguments based on military or political expediency. They constitute a professional challenge to a limited group of people, as does a supersonic airplane, the Mt. Palomar telescope, an unconquered mountain peak or a sandstorm observed on Mars.

If this were all, one could well take space flight or leave it alone. The anthropological challenge of space flight, however, goes much deeper. Its perspective and meaning, which alone lend magnetic appeal, can be derived only from the long-range aspects, which align it alongside the highlights of life on this planet.

Realism of Vision Needed

We must be realistic, but there is a wrong kind of realism, timid and static, which tells man to live for his existence alone and not to rock the boat. The kind of realism we need is the realism of vision—the realism of a Columbus, of our Constitution, of a Benjamin Franklin, of an Albert Einstein, of a Konstantin Ziolkowsky and of a Hermann Oberth.

This is the realism which lives by our first law, the very foundation of man's development—the law that states that we are free to grow in this grand universe of ours unless we put the yoke around our own necks. In this spirit, it will not be too difficult to deal with the immediate utilities which rightfully provide the formal justification for each subsequent phase of astronautical development.

However we look at astronautics, it is impossible not to feel its challenge to human destiny. For this reason, space travel needs, and will find, the support of all civilized nations as we gradually and painfully move into the cosmic age of man.

again just a beginning, no matter how advanced it may appear to us.

If all the evidence is in, future generations may find solutions to the problem of living elsewhere in the Solar system, or even in interstellar space, thereby giving space flight its ultimate anthropological meaning. It is not very important that we cannot yet specify in more than a general way the utility of living elsewhere in space, because we are about as competent to judge this as Democritus was to judge the utility of atomic knowledge which he so diligently pursued.

This does not mean that consideration of utility should be overlooked. On the contrary. However, astronautics, like all endeavors of large scope, has both an immediate, utilitarian aspect, and a long-range, fundamental aspect. It is not only sensible, but imperative, to establish the utility of a particular project such as an artificial satellite, a lunar probe or an artificial comet.

'The Woman on Mars'

This dramatic presentation was Presidential candidate Lyndon LaRouche's 1987 bold proposal of a mission to colonize Mars, and to envision how such a 40-year mission would transform the United States.[1]

What I am about to present to you are the highlights of present U.S. plans for establishing a permanent colony on Mars by approximately the year 2027 A.D. The plans to be outlined here are based on the two somewhat similar, but slightly differing versions of the plan as developed by various U.S. specialists. One plan is that first presented at a June 1985 conference in honor of the space pioneer, Krafft Ehricke, who died at the end of 1984. The second plan, is one drafted by the National Commission on Space, and presented approximately a year after the Krafft Ehricke conference. This presentation will emphasize the approach laid out at the Krafft Ehricke memorial conference, but it will also make use of important features of the proposals by the Commission on Space.

For this purpose, I ask you to come with me, in your imagination, to a Wednesday in September, in the year 2036 A.D., nine years after the Mars colony has been founded. Starting from an imaginary television broadcast to Earth at 1800 hours London time, that day, let us look from that day and year, back to the time of the United States' adoption of the Mars colonization project, and trace each major step of the project from the year 1989, up to the year 2027, the year the first permanent colony on Mars is finally established.

Those who have worked to prepare this presentation, have thought that we must use our powers of imagination in this way. It is thought, that we must focus attention on our destination as we outline each step of a journey. It seems to us, that that is the only way this project, and its importance for all mankind, can be properly understood.

To present the project in this way, it is necessary to include some imaginary political figures and political events, so that we might present this as a story. However, the technical facts we use here represent the scientific and related facts of the Mars colonization plan as those facts exist today.

* * *

The BBC television studio's clock says that it is 1800 hours in London, on Wednesday, September 3, 2036 A.D. From 55 million miles away, on Mars, a televised image travels nearly 5 minutes across space, to be picked up by the giant geostationary receiver hovering over the South Atlantic, from where the signal is relayed to other satellites, reaching waiting disk-antennas around the world. A woman's face appears on the BBC screen.

The woman on the screen is in her late thirties. The sight of her familiar features brings expressions of admiration to the viewing audiences now receiving this live broadcast around most of the world. She is Dr. Ellen Jones, chief executive of the Mars colony, and the daughter of the famous space pioneer, Dr. Walter Jones, who headed the U.S.A.'s Mars-colonization program from 2008 until his retirement in 2027.

"I bring you greetings from your 683,648 relatives and friends living here on Mars, and some very good news," she begins. "Our astrophysicists agree, that with our latest series of observations at our Cyclops III radiotelescope, we have solved at least a good part of the mystery of what you know as black holes. We are convinced that we are at the verge of fundamentally new ideas about how our universe works."

The TV audience followed her 5-minute televised report with a scientific interest which would have been unimaginable when the Mars-colonization mission was first launched by the U.S., back in March 1989.

---

1. LaRouche's script was intended for film and slide-show presentation. It was the basis for a still-remembered half-hour television broadcast of that name, during LaRouche's 1988 campaign for the Democratic Presidential nomination. Illustrations here were originally published in *21st Century Science and Technology*, Winter 1996-97.

The 1990s flights of transatmospheric craft up to stations in low-Earth orbit, had revived the spirit of the popularity of space-exploration from the Apollo-project period of the 1960s. After Earth's first geostationary space-terminal had been completed near the end of the 1990s, manned flights to the Moon had soon become routine. Over the 1990s, the point was reached that every schoolchild, not only in the U.S., Europe, and Japan, but throughout the world, demanded to know everything possible about space.

Beginning the 1990s, fewer and fewer university students attended courses in the social sciences, as the physical sciences, including space biology, took over the classrooms almost completely. Even at preschool ages, more and more children, asked what gift they wished for Christmas, would answer, "a telescope." As the industrialization of the Moon began near the end of the 21st century's first decade, to look up was to express optimism about the human race's future. Space and the spirit of adventure became one and the same.

There had been a deeper quality of changes in attitudes. What had been the most popular competitive sports of the 20th century became less popular, and achievement in swimming, track and field, and mountain-climbing, the most popular features of physical education programs. "Keeping in shape for space travel," was the value which more and more attached to physical education.

Twentieth-century man would be astonished to know the new way in which "spirit of adventure" was translated during the early decades of the 21st. Some things 20th-century man would have recognized. Being the first to set foot on some planetary body, was of course a commonplace fantasy among children and youth. The difference was, most teenagers, and some much younger, already knew the real purpose of space exploration. That purpose was, to acquire knowledge which the human race needed, and could not gain without scientific exploration of our universe in a way which could not be done without traveling far beyond Earth's orbit. The idea of adventure, was not a matter of simply getting to some strange place out there. Exciting adventure, was to participate in making some exciting new discovery in space, which would be useful to the majority of the human race remaining back here on Earth.

So, those children and youth gobbled up every bit of information they could, with the purpose being to understand what kind of knowledge mankind was seeking out there.

NASA/Bill Ingalls

Schoolchildren in Tampa, Fla. outfitted for a mission on their "Space Shuttle" bus, which is designed inside like a Shuttle orbiter.

The last two years, 2025-2026, just before the building of the first permanent colony on Mars, had seen the most rapid transformation in popular values here on Earth.

The TV screens had been filled often with images of those giant spacecraft, each much larger than a 20th century ocean liner, taking off from the vicinity of Earth's geostationary space-terminal, in flotillas of five or more, each seeming to thunder silently in the near-vacuum under 1-gravity acceleration. By then, a permanent space-terminal was being constantly manned in Mars orbit. The televised broadcasts from that terminal showed the monstrous spacecraft arriving. Earth's television screens showed the gradual accumulation of that vast amount of material in Mars orbit, waiting for the day it would descend to Mars's surface. TV viewers on Earth saw the first craft, designed to descend and rise through the thin atmosphere of Mars, and saw views of the approaching Mars surface from the cockpit, through the eyes of the cameras.

A great anticipation built up throughout Earth's population during those last two preparatory years. Then, Earth went through what was afterward described as the "sleepless year," as the first city was assembled on Mars, during 2027. Audiences on Earth demanded to see every step of the construction relayed back here. Nearly everyone on Earth became thus a "sidewalk superintendent" for as many available hours as his or her sleep-starved eyes could be kept open. On waking, it was the same. The daily successes reported from Mars were discussed as widely and in as much detail as 20th century sports fans debated the details of a weekend's football play.

By then, holographic projections had become as economical and commonplace as personal computers had been during the 1980s. Building a synthetic holographic model of the solar system, and constructing a powered-flight trajectory, such as one between Earth and Mars, became quite literally child's play. A child's parent could purchase a packaged program at a local store, and the child often insisted that this be done. Turning on one's system, and updating the positions of the planets and the course of a space-flotilla flight in progress, became a habit with many. The same was done with various stages of the construction of the first permanent colony. Whatever was seen on the TV screen, was something one wished to reconstruct. The passive TV watching of the 20th century had come to an end.

The first large-aperture radiotelescopes had been constructed a million or so miles from Mars, as soon as the manned orbiting space-terminal had been completed. The system of observatories and space-laboratories associated with them, was expanded rapidly, once the first 100,000 permanent colonists had begun to settle in. Popular fascination here on Earth, shifted its focus somewhat from the Mars colony itself, to these new projects.

It was such a worldwide audience which sat or stood, absorbed with every sentence of Dr. Jones's 5-minute report, either as it was being broadcast, or when morning reached them a few hours later. Throughout the planet, over the course of that Wednesday and Thursday, there was the eerily joyful sense that humanity had reached a major milestone in the existence of our species. It would be said, in later decades, that on that day in 2036, the Age of Reason had truly begun.

At the beginning of the 1950s, space pioneers such as Wernher von Braun had begun working out the specifications for manned flights to Mars. One leading Peenemünde veteran, Krafft Ehricke, had been certain that the United States could have sent a manned exploratory flight to Mars as early as the 1980s. Unfortunately, near the end of 1966, the United States had cut back massively on its aerospace programs. Presidents Johnson and Nixon did not eliminate President Kennedy's popular commitment to a manned landing on the Moon from the NASA program, but most of the other aerospace projects, such as nuclear-powered propulsion development, were cut back, and cut back savagely as soon as the program of initial Moon landings had been completed. Krafft Ehricke continued toward his completion of the design for industrialization of the Moon, but he died in 1984, his work nearly completed on paper, with no visible prospect that the U.S. would resume such a commitment during the foreseeable future.

It was not until shortly after Ehricke's death that a renewed U.S. commitment to colonization of Mars appeared. The proposal for a permanent colony on Mars as early as the middle 2020s, was a featured presentation at a Virginia conference held in honor of Krafft's memory, in June 1985. Nearly a year after that, the National Commission on Space adopted the same target date, and its proposal was endorsed, although without significant funding, by President Ronald Reagan. However, the Mars colonization project was a featured part of the January 1989 State of the Union address of the new President. During March of 1989 a U.S. Moon-Mars Colonization Commission was established. During that month, the Congress rushed through approval of treaty agreements which the President negotiated with Japan and Western European governments, establishing these allies as partners in the U.S.-sponsored Moon-Mars Colonization Project, following on similar international agreements which had led to the construction of the space stations of the 1990s.

Popular enthusiasm for the project was so great, that the President was able to secure a $5 billion initial budgetary allotment for the new project. Japan matched this with a sizably increased allotment to its own aerospace program shortly after that. Confident that changes in U.S. policies were going to bring the world out of what threatened to become a major depression, Western European governments came close, in total, to matching Japan's budgetary allotment.

The successive phases of the Moon-Mars colonization project were agreed upon that same year.

It was quickly understood, that planting a permanent colony on Mars is a far different sort of undertaking than sending a manned exploratory vessel to visit Mars. Leaders recognized, that to establish a colony of even a few hundred members of scientific parties on Mars would require a very large complex of production workers, agriculturalists, and so forth.

Back at the end of the 1980s, most citizens and politicians did not yet understand the significance of the fact that Mars is an average 55 million miles distance from Earth during the period one might ordinarily think of making such a flight. To sustain just a few hundreds persons there, was, by late 20th century standards, a tremendous number of ton-miles of freight to be shipped from Earth annually. The scientists understood this immediately, of course, but it required a lot of effort to make this clear to most of the politicians, and to popular opinion.

NASA

Astronauts are collecting Mars samples and conducting scientific observations, while a dust storm is approaching the cratered area near the landing site. In the background is Olympus Mons.

The scientists realized very soon, that we should plan to put not just hundreds of scientists, engineers, and technicians, on Mars. The purpose for going to Mars in the first place was scientific investigations. The main purpose was to build a system of enormous radio telescopes in the region of space near Mars, and to conduct the construction, maintenance, and improvements of these observatories from bases both in Mars orbit and on the surface of the planet. Using U.S. experience in demonstration tests of trained human individuals' efficiency working in low-gravity Earth-orbit gained from the 1980s Space Shuttle and the 1990s space stations, it was estimated, that to construct as many observatories as Earth would need to explore the universe in as fine detail as must be done from Mars orbit, would require hundreds of thousands of man-hours each year. This figure included estimates on the number of days a year a human being could safely work in a very low-gravity field.

The scientists estimated, that the cost of keeping a research worker alive on Mars adds up to a total amount of equipment more than 10 times that required to sustain a scientist in the middle of the Sahara or Antarctica. This did not include the estimated costs of transporting all that tonnage from Earth to Mars. The scientists explained to the politicians, "Mars is a very cold place by Earth standards, with a very thin atmosphere, a shortage of known water-supplies, and a lower gravity than Earth. People living on Mars must live in man-made environments under protective domes. The costs of maintaining those domes, of maintaining water supplies, of maintaining the atmosphere, and maintaining an acceptable temperature within the artificial climate, are enormous by Earth standards." The biggest factor of cost those scientists had to consider was the cost of energy; they estimated that more than 10 times the amount of energy must be available, per person, on Mars, than the energy directly consumed by research teams in the Sahara or Antartica.

They decided that the basic source of energy used on Mars would have to be thermonuclear fusion, as it already was on the Moon. They pointed out, that the Mars colony would need very concentrated sources of industrial energy, to enable the colony to produce food and to sustain itself with the largest part of its requirements in materials.

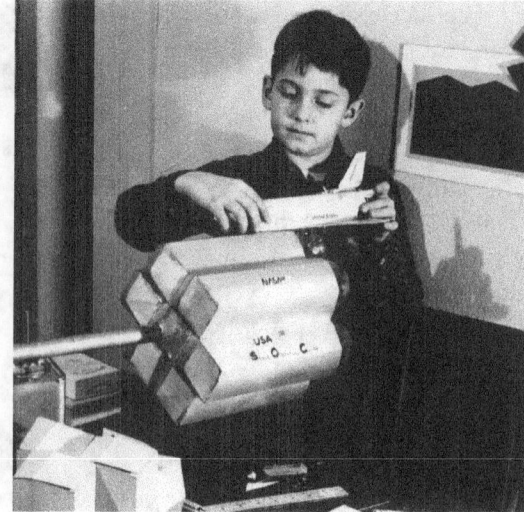

Philip Ulanowsky

Carlos de Hoyos

Children spent their time building models of everything to do with space—from spacecraft to fusion power plants.

So, it was agreed that the way to sustain our teams of research workers on Mars, was to build a local supporting economy on Mars. They estimated that between a quarter and a half million total population would be the minimum size for a successful colony. They thought that this might be sufficient, if we gave Mars the new generation of industrial technologies which were in the initial development stages on Earth back during the 1980s.

They saw, that to get that number of people to Mars, together with all that was needed to start up a colony of this size, was plainly impossible using the methods worked out for sending a manned exploratory flight to Mars. To lift that amount of weight from Earth's surface, up into high-Earth-orbit, by conventional rocket methods in use in the 1980s, was beyond possible limits of cost. Even if the cost were greatly reduced by improved methods of liftoff, the amount of weight which would have to be lifted to deliver the requirements of a quarter to half a million Mars colonists from Earth, was still so costly as to be out of the question.

The politicians had imagined, wrongly, that starting a colony on Mars was like establishing a research base-station in the Antarctic. The politicians imagined, that the technologies developed for sending a manned team of explorers could be expanded to transport a much larger number of colonists. The scientists had to make clear why this idea was badly mistaken.

First of all, human bodies are designed to function under one Earth gravity, or at least something near to that. The human body might be able to adapt to gravi-

ties a large fraction of those on Earth, but long flights at nearly zero-gravity are very risky, and were thought to be quite possibly fatal. So, the idea of sending people to Mars in the way we sent astronauts to the Moon, was ruled out. The best way they knew to create the effect of one Earth gravity in spacecraft was to have that spacecraft constantly powered by one Earth gravity's worth of acceleration, or at least a large fraction of one Earth gravity, creating an effect very much like the way a person's weight increases when being accelerated upward in a 20th century elevator. The scientists pointed out, that powered flight at one-Earth-gravity acceleration, made possible new kinds of trajectory-paths between Mars and Earth, and reduced the travel time enormously.

Some pointed out that this might be possible with ion engines powered by fission reactors. It was agreed that thermonuclear fusion would be far superior in several ways. They explained that fusion energy was the form of energy production which would be needed on Mars, in any case, and that fission-powered ion engines would still take too long to make the trip to Mars. The problem they tackled was convincing the politicians that the needed development of fusion energy had to be completed before the Mars trips began.

It was decided, at the beginning, that the main part of solving the problem of lifting weight into geostationary Earth orbit from Earth's surface, would be industrializing the Moon. Provided fusion power could be established on the Moon, they guessed that more than 90 percent of the total weight of large space-vessels, could be produced on the Moon, and lifted into Moon orbit at a small fraction of the cost of producing these materials on Earth. The same thing would apply to most of the materials sent to Mars to construct the first stages of a permanent colony. Space vessels to Mars, could be assembled in either Moon-orbit or Earth-orbit, and launched from either place. The scientists decided, that using a rocket to get beyond the Earth's atmosphere is like designing an aircraft to fly under water. The idea of using a transatmospheric aircraft to get above the atmosphere, had been under discussion for decades, and preliminary designs were fairly well advanced during the course of the 1980s. It was decided to push the development of transatmospheric craft, to build up a network of low-orbiting space-terminals. This would provide the cheapest possible way of moving large numbers of people, and large amounts of freight, up beyond the atmosphere. It would also be the cheapest and safest way to bring people down from orbit to airports on the Earth.

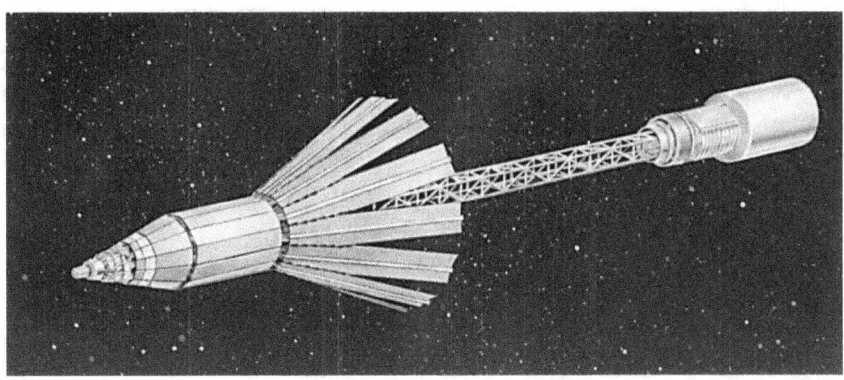

NASA

One early design for a space nuclear power system that would provide sufficient power for Earth-orbiting spacecraft, a lunar colony, or a piloted Mars mission.

By that time, there were already designs for what were then called "space ferries." These "space ferries" would carry people and materials over the distance from the low-orbiting terminals, to the locations of the main space terminals, in Earth's geostationary orbit. These geostationary terminals became the locations at which technicians assembled the craft used for regular travel between Earth and Moon.

So, on August **, 2000, the first routine travel between Earth and the Moon was begun. Some of the astronauts grumbled, complaining that they had become high-paid airline pilots. It was pretty much routine. It was policy, that the pilot made only a few round-trips between the Moon and Earth-orbit, before being sent back to Earth for rest and rehabilitation, although the main Earth space terminals already had a one-Earth-gravity artificial environment at that time. After a few trips, the space-pilots would board a regular bus-run of the space ferry at the space-station, get off at a low-orbiting terminal, and catch the next transatmospheric flight back to Earth.

Few people living in 2036 remember this obscure event, but back in 1986, the United States sent two pilots to prove that a propeller aircraft could make a nonstop trip around the world. Most scientists thought the trip was a silly way to waste money for no useful purpose. The only reason one would mention that obscure flight in 2036, would be to show the kinds of problems the scientists faced in explaining space-colonization to the politicians and voters.

Imagine a propeller aircraft, the combined weight of whose engines, fuselage, and pilots are nearly zero. In other words, how far can a pound of gasoline fly itself, given the efficiencies of propeller aircraft? So, this obscure flight was designed, making the weights of engines, fuselage, and pilots, as small a percentage of the weight of the plane's maximum fuel load as possible. What did the flight prove? Nothing that a qualified aeronautics engineer could not have proven with an electronic hand calculator.

The problem, back in 1989, was to explain to the politicians and public how this same problem, of total weight to fuel weight, limited the possibilities for getting into space, and affected the costs of getting a pound of weight into space. As everyone knows today, the farther a vessel moves from a planet's strongest gravitational pull, the less fuel it costs to accelerate a pound of weight.

The politicians got the point. The system of getting into space, from the Earth's surface to the geostationary space terminal, and to the Moon's orbit, was a kind of pyramid. The distance from Earth's geostationary terminal to Moon-orbit, was the tip of the pyramid. The transatmosopheric system, between the Earth's surface and the low-orbiting terminals, was the broadest strip of the pyramid. The space ferries, moving back and forth between the low-orbiting terminals and the geostationary terminal, were the middle section of the pyramid.

One of the biggest obstacles the space program had to overcome, was the massive prejudice most of the

Lunar industrialization was necessary to produce and send materials to Mars, for its first permanent colony. Here, a lunar resource processing plant, with two space nuclear power units in the background.

politicians and public had built up against nuclear fission over nearly 20 years, between 1970 and the time the project began, in 1989. The political factor, of fear of nuclear radiation, was far more important than the engineering problems involved in using nuclear fission safely as a power source for aircraft and space vehicles. This prejudice was a major engineering difficulty, since nuclear fission gives much more power per unit of weight than chemical fuels. In all travel, the ratio of total weight to weight of the maximum fuel load, is the most important of the economic limits to be faced.

However, by that time, thermonuclear fusion as a power source was nearly a reality. Fusion is vastly more efficient as a fuel user, than nuclear fission. So, nuclear fission was the power source for regular flights between Earth-orbit and Moon-orbit during those early years after 2000, but its uses for other modes of flight was avoided.

To get from Earth-Moon to Mars, required us to develop another pyramid, with the base of the pyramid running from Earth's geostationary orbit to the Moon's production facilities, the tip of the pyramid reaching Mars surface, and the distance between the base-line and Mars-orbit the lower portion of the pyramid's volume.

A third pyramid was designed. The base of this pyramid was on Mars's surface. Just as on Earth, we must move passengers and some freight from Mars's surface into Mars-orbit. From there, in Mars-orbit, the pyramid branches in two directions. One direction leads back to Earth-orbit. The other direction was powered travel, as from Earth-orbit to Moon-orbit, to and from the radio telescopes and space laboratories constructed in the general vicinity of Mars.

Those three pyramids became the fundamental design of the system of transportation as a whole.

Once the first of the two pyramids had been designed, the key bottleneck next to be mastered, was production on the Moon.

Quite clearly, the scientists could not think of building a 19th-century-style metals industry on the Moon. The combustion of oxygen, which had been the basis for metalworking on Earth deep into the 20th century, was not a workable proposition on the Moon, even if a combustible fuel could be found. Only three sources of industrial energy could be found. Electricity could be generated in various ways, or nuclear fission or thermonuclear fusion could be used. Just past the turn of the century, the fusionable isotope, helium-3 was being mined on the Moon.

Krafft Ehricke had worked out a nuclear-fission economy for the Moon, but it was realized that a thermonuclear-fusion economy would be far better. For the rest, the standard handbooks of physics and chemistry already existing in the 1980s were most helpful.

The policy decided upon was this. As every schoolchild knows his ABCs in 2036, production of inorganic materials is a matter of what most back in the 1980s still referred to as the available temperatures of production processes. If the highest industrial temperatures then in general use, could be increased by an absolute factor of slightly less than 10 times existing modes, there was no material in the solar system which cannot be reduced to a plasma form under such conditions. Back in the 1980s, we had only two ways in sight for doing this efficiently, thermonuclear fusion and coherent electromagnetic pulses of high frequency, and very high energy-density cross-section of impact upon targeted materials.

The problem which the project's leaders faced then,

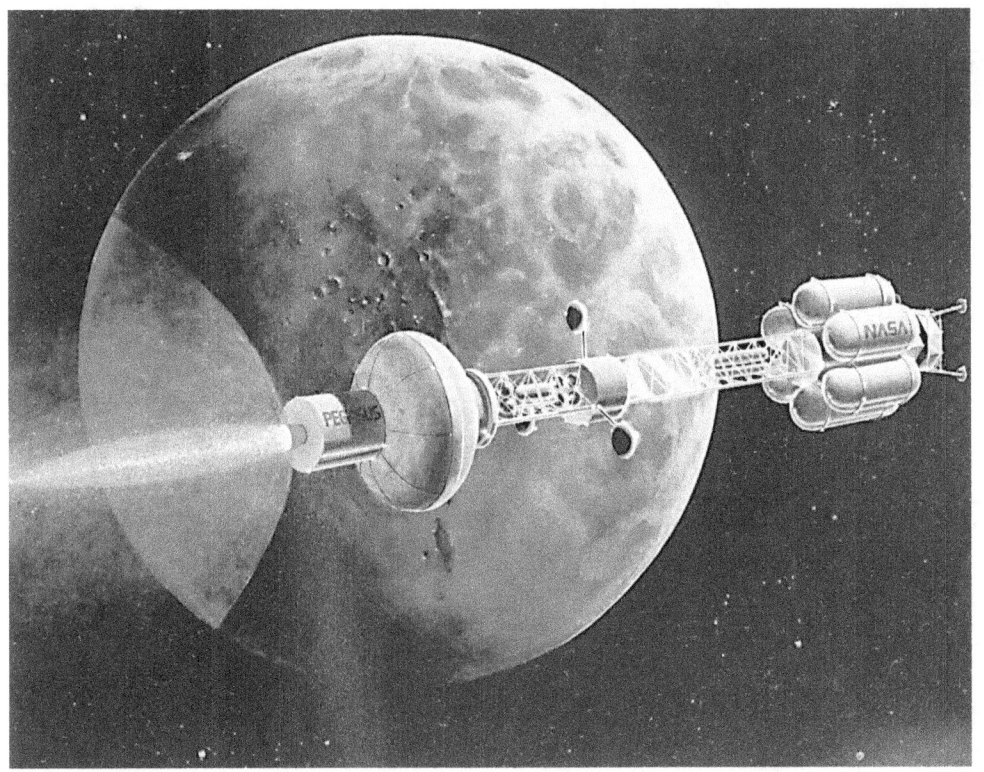

NASA

One of the new plasma applications is magnetoplasmadynamic thrusters for use in cargo vehicle propulsion. This artist's drawing shows a high performance electric propulsion cargo vehicle approaching Mars.

als-production problems we faced on the Moon, greatly accelerated our civilization's development of newer types of ceramics. We did not have the development of ceramic materials of anomalous crystalline structures on the list of project requirements at the start, but once we recognized the advantages of materials so novel to us at that time, we added the forced development of these technologies to our project.

In the same way, we were forced to develop the early varieties of laser machine-tools in general use in 2036, to be able to machine these new materials. Our project brought the techniques of electromagnetic isotope separation up to a level of refinement still considered modern today.

It was the success of these breakthroughs in fusion,

was that if we reduce material to its plasma state, how do we handle it? The answer is familiar to every schoolchild in 2036, but it was a major problem for the scientists back in 1989. The key to the solution was obviously lessons learned in experimental efforts to develop thermonuclear fusion as a source of power.

If was clear from the beginning of the project, that if the schedules set for Mars colonization were to be realized, it was indispensable to accelerate thermonuclear fusion development and development of techniques associated with high-frequency lasers and particle beams. The development of the gamma-ray laser was given much higher priority through these decisions. The decision was made, to achieve what were called then "second generation" thermonuclear fusion technologies by the middle of the 21st century's first decade, and to put accelerated efforts behind mastery of techniques for production of materials using electromagnetically confined plasmas.

The fact that we were obliged to force the development of advanced technologies then on the horizon, in order that we might solve the materi-

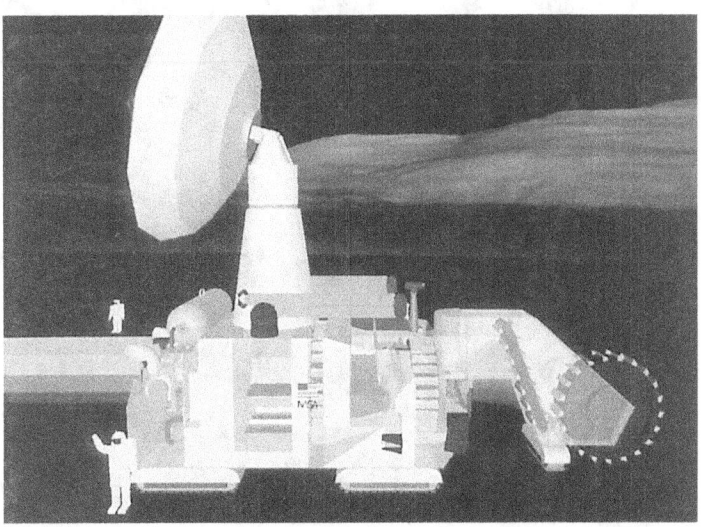

John Andrews/Fusion Technology Institute, University of Wisconsin

There are about 1 million tons of helium-3—a rare isotope of helium, which can be used as fusion fuel—trapped on and near the surface of the Moon. This Lunar Mark-II is a mobile robotic miner designed to process the soil, extract the helium, redeposit the processed soil, and move on. The University of Wisconsin device has a soil processing rate of 556 tons per hour.

The process of lunar industrialization prepared the way for colonizing Mars. Here, a lunar resource processing pilot plant, designed to develop the technologies used for collection, analysis, and both mechanical and electrochemical separation of lunar surface resources; for production of materials needed for life support and propulsion (such as oxygen); and fabrication and construction of structural elements.

Illustration by Krafft A. Ehricke

Christmas 2031 in Selenopolis—the Moon city envisioned by space scientist Krafft Ehricke. At left is the "Hall of the Astronauts." At right, an elevated monorail train. Behind the transparent insulation is a nodal dome with supplies and life support and climatizing equipment. At the rear is a domed tropical habitat sector.

lasers, and very high energy-density production processes, which made the industrialization of the Moon such a brilliant success. It was by perfecting these

methods and processes for the industrialization of the Moon that we solved in advance the major problems we would have otherwise faced during the initial colonization of Mars. The building up of the Moon's industrialization was the major factor forcing us to delay the beginning of Mars colonization until 2027. Had we not developed the technologies needed for industrialization of the Moon, as we did, the colonization of Mars would have been delayed by a decade or more.

Some of the 1985-1986 plans included a heavy emphasis on new directions in biology, but without the desperate fight Earth had to mobilize against the AIDS pandemic, it is doubtful that many supporters of our Mars colonization project would have been won over to supporting this line of research to the degree which later proved necessary, once the Mars colonization had begun. So, today, we are able to incorporate the benefits of this research into designs of systems for manned deep-space explorations, and have overcome most of the fears of possible strange diseases which might be encountered, or might develop, in our further explorations and colonizations of space.

It was not until the late 1990s, that the last significant political opposition to the costliness of the Mars-colonization project was overcome.

We began the project in 1989, under what might seem to have been the worst economic conditions for such an undertaking. Over the preceding 25 years, most of the world had been caught in a long process of economic decline, which we described then as a drift into a "postindustrial society." In many of the then-industrialized nations, the average income of households had fallen to about 70 percent of the real purchasing power of 1966 and 1967. Entire industries which had existed during the 1960s, had either been wiped out, or nearly so, in many of these nations. The basic economic infrastructure, such things as water management and sanitation systems, general transportation of freight, energy systems, and educational and health care systems, were in a state of advanced decay. To cover over the collapse of incomes, a massive spiral of borrowing had occurred in all sectors of government, production, and households; a terrible financial crisis had built up.

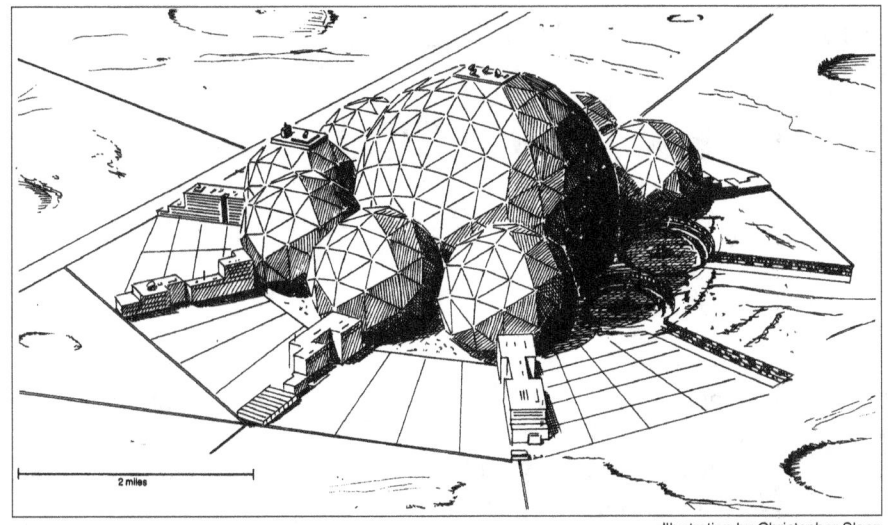

Illustration by Christopher Sloan

Kepleropolis, the first Mars colony, is depicted here in the construction phase. Its main dome, 1 mile in diameter, is built in a crater. Surrounding the main dome are 10 smaller domes, each able to support neighborhoods of 50,000 individuals. The ecliptic of the dome is at ground level. On the surface level is a large educational and recreational park. Immediately below are administrative offices, and on levels below that are transporation and storage facilities and a central fusion power plant. An astronomical observatory and communications station is on top of the main dome.

Those who pushed the Mars colonization project the most, including the President of the United States, did not view the project as a way of spending a large surplus of wealth. It was seen by them as a way of helping to revive a decaying economy, and also a way of showing all mankind that our species has meaningful opportunities for present and future generations, opportunities as limitless as the universe itself.

At first, many grumbled political objections against the large sums of money spent. As the citizens saw new industries and employment opportunities opening up as a result of the Mars project, the political support for the project grew. Over the course of the first 10 years, the project grew in importance as a technological stimulant to the growth of economies. Then, the first decade of the 21st century, there were waves of revolutionary improvements in methods of production; many of these benefits were the direct result of using the new space technologies in everyday production back on Earth. The political opposition to the project's cost vanished.

One of the first of the developing nations to join Japan, the U.S., and Western Europe, in the project, was India. The next were Argentina and Brazil. The project's leaders and sponsors showed wisdom in encouraging participation in their own programs by young scientists from many nations. The fact that we may be so confident that general war has disappeared from Earth in 2036,

can be credited to the Mars colonization project to a large degree. The rate of technological advancement and increase of wealth in the nations which undertook the project from the start, has been such that no potential adversary would think of attacking them.

As it became clearer to everyone that there were going to be large permanent colonies in Mars during the middle of the 21st century, the general idea of developing the worst deserts of Earth worked its way into policies of governments. Africa, whose population-level collapsed by more than 100 million during the course of the AIDS pandemic, is growing again, and not only the Sahel region, but large stretches of the Sahara are blooming areas with new, modern cities.

No one talks of overpopulation any more. The idea of transforming the Earth-sized moon of Saturn, Titan, into a new colony, beginning 40 to 50 years from now, is already more popular than the colonization of Mars was, back during the late 1980s. Titan's atmosphere is poisonous, but we can foresee ourselves gaining the kinds of technologies needed to Earth-form a planetary body of that sort. The strongest voice for this is coming from the Mars colonists, who now say that they find everything delightful on Mars but its uncomfortably low gravity. There is also big pressure for such new major space projects from circles tied closely to the Moon industrialization program; they say that Moon industries are ripe for a major new challenge.

The Mars colony will be almost self-sustaining within another 10 years. No one on Earth worries any more about Earth's continued subsidy of the colony; who doubts today, that the economic benefits are already vastly greater than the amounts we have spent. There are now over 200 spacecraft traveling back and forth between the orbits of Earth and Mars, and with each journey, more going to Mars than returning. We expect the population to reach over a million within a few years. We wonder if more than a handful living back in the late 1980s dreamed how much their decisions would change not only the world, but the solar system, for the better, within two generations.

KRAFFT EHRICKE AND LYNDON LAROUCHE

'Lifting the Human Species Out of Its Ordinary Existence'

by Megan Beets

March 20—Today we are in the midst of a pivotal moment in history, which will decide much about the fate of mankind for the coming century, and beyond. Despite the chaos being fomented in the United States against the Trump administration, this moment is an incredibly optimistic one. The system that has controlled the world for centuries, the system of geopolitics, has collapsed. Along with it have collapsed (unless we are foolish enough to cling to them) the failed ideas and axioms that have governed how people think—what they value, what they believe to be true, or powerful, and what policies they will accept.

For example: the notion that money is equivalent to wealth. There is more money in the financial system than ever before in mankind's history, yet look at how far the standard of living for the average American has fallen compared to 50 years ago, or even 10 years ago! Add to that the spike in the death rate in the United States due to drug overdoses and suicides. Take the idea that one nation's rise is a threat to every other nation—a central tenet of geopolitics. This lie is being completely overturned by China's "One Belt One Road" policy of win-win cooperation, which is based on the *common* aims and *common* good of all nations, and has already begun to revolutionize the economies of Eurasia and Africa.

Perhaps the biggest, most all-encompassing axiom which has polluted people's ability to think straight for half a century now is that there are "limits to growth," an upper limit to the increase of the human population—meaning that ultimately there is a ceiling to

Krafft Ehricke (right) with a colleague.

man's ability to progress. There are many manifestations of this fallacy: the belief that population growth is inherently bad; that we should strive to reduce our impact on the planet; that human activity loots the Earth's resources and our development destroys the environment; or that we are in competition with other people for a fixed amount of resources. The common effect of these variations on a theme is to make us *small*; we think small, we act small, and we dismiss the kinds of methods that change history as "impossible." Often, people are not conscious about how their thinking has been affected by being part of a society which has operated this way for fifty years—but it *has*, and for most people there is the subconscious belief that we can not actually progress forever—that at some point, mankind will run into a limit which we cannot surpass.

That limitation happens to be true for all animals, but it's *not* true for humans. Not only is there no limit to our power to grow, but we are *supposed* to grow; we are *supposed* to expand and increase our population, and to consume more than our ancestors. That consumption is not for its own sake, but rather reflects a unique power of the human mind. Think about what kinds of things we today consume more of than those who came before us, or more interestingly, what kinds of things we consume that our ancestors *could not* have, because they did not yet exist!

To take one example, in the United States we consume much more water per capita today than people did 200 years ago. Why? Because people are wasteful, or take longer showers? No! Domestic water use today is

EIRNS/Stuart Lewis

Lyndon LaRouche addressing the Schiller Institute Memorial Conference in Reston, Va, June 16, 1985.

less than 10% of total water consumption. Much more, almost 80%, is used in power generation and agriculture. The amount of land under cultivation and the amount of irrigated farmland is *many* times more per capita now than several of centuries ago, which means more food production, including in places where it could not exist apart from man's intervention. The amount of water used in electricity generation is *infinitely* more than in 1800!

Now take a more interesting example: how much uranium was consumed per capita in 1800? Almost none. Why? Because it had virtually no use before the discovery of the powers of the nucleus at the end of the nineteenth century. Today, uranium generates power for millions of people and industries.

We *create* new things that our ancestors could not consume, as a byproduct of new discoveries. In that way, we evolve as a species as no animal can. The biosphere *as a whole* evolves to higher levels of complexity and energy, but it does so through a process of turnover of species—some go extinct while new ones emerge. However, human beings do not evolve biologically; we evolve *voluntarily and creatively*, through a process of discovery of new universal principles.

That is the purpose of economic policy: to shape the activity within and among nations to optimize the potential for new discoveries, and their application to develop mankind. That is what the space program is about.

Krafft Ehricke: A Creative Identity

Krafft Ehricke, the great space visionary and one of the key founders of the space program, is someone who took on the voluntary evolution of the human species as a personal responsibility, and as the meaning of his identity.

He stood firmly against the "limits to growth" ideology, and asserted that man has a higher nature than the beasts:

We are cosmic creatures by substance, by the energy on which we operate and by the restless mind that ceaselessly metabolizes information from the infinitesimal to the infinite and, on the infrastructure of knowledge, pursues its moral and social aspirations for a larger and better world against many odds. Through intelligences like ourselves, the universe, and we in it, move into the focus of self-recognition; metal ore is turned into information processing computers, satellites and deep-space probes; and atoms are fused as in stars. I cannot imagine a more foreboding, apocalyptic vision of the future than a mankind endowed with cosmic powers but condemned to solitary confinement on one small planet.[1]

Ehricke was born in Berlin on March 24, 1917, and from a very early age was fascinated with the notion of man traveling into space. In 1929, he saw the Fritz Lang movie *Frau im Mond* (*The Woman in the Moon*), and was so fascinated that he went back to see it many more times. "It impressed me enormously. I was at that time twelve years old, and it shocked me into the awareness, all of a sudden: You might be able to leave this planet, to open a new world! And since my interest already at that time was in history and astronomy and the evolu-

---

1. All Krafft Ehricke citations are from Marsha Freeman, *Krafft Ehricke's Extraterrestrial Imperative*, Apogee Books, 2008.

tion of man, in a very simple way, it kind of gave me a tremendous impulse to interest myself in space. And after two or three years in reading books, and so forth, I became firmly determined that this is an area of technology I wanted to devote my life to."

During World War II he was drafted into the army, and in 1941 was sent to the eastern front as commander of a tank unit. Luckily, some patents he had filed on rocket technology came to the attention of General Walter Dornberger, who was then assembling a group of rocket scientists at Peenemünde, the Army Experimental Station on the Baltic coast, and Ehricke was redeployed. It was here that the space age began.[2]

Krafft remembered very vividly Oct. 3, 1942, the day the first rocket was successfully sent into space:

> Those were the "wild west" days of rocketry and space flight. You didn't have to be miles away. You could almost stand beside the rocket, and I was on the roof of one of those high-rise buildings, actually looking down to the launch complex, just a few hundred meters distance. And then came the countdown and ignition. The system lifted off with a roar, it lifted up straight, and, of course, we all screamed with delight. It hadn't exploded on the launch complex. The guidance seemed to work… it looked like a fiery sword going into the sky. Then came the enormous roar—the whole sky seemed to vibrate. This kind of unearthly roaring sound was something human ears had never heard [before].
>
> You know, it's very hard to describe what you feel when you stand on the threshold of a whole new era, of a whole new age that you know will be coming. It's like those people must have felt—Columbus or Magellan—that for the first time, saw entire new worlds, and knew the world would never be the same after this… This is the feeling many of us had.
>
> For me, it was absolutely overwhelming. I almost fell off the roof, I was so excited.
>
> When we came down together, we congratu-

A V-2 rocket launched in Summer 1943.

Bundesarchiv

lated ourselves. We knew the Space Age had begun and Dr. Dornberger made a very moving speech at the time, and said, "Well, this is the key to the universe. This is the first day of the Space Age."

At the end of the war, Ehricke along with many of his colleagues, such as Wernher von Braun, worked very hard to make sure they could surrender to the Americans, rather than the Soviets, and in 1946 Krafft came to the United States under a contract with the U.S. Army to bring the rocket technology developed in Germany to the United States.

Inventing Mankind's Future

Krafft Ehricke was a brilliant engineer. For example, he was the person who figured out, on assignment from Wernher von Braun, that the use of liquid hydro-

---

2. Ehricke learned later that after his departure, his entire tank unit was wiped out.

gen, a much higher-thrust fuel than safer-to-handle alternatives, could be feasible, thus allowing much heavier payloads to be taken into orbit. The hydrogen-fueled Centaur upper-stage—which has carried everything from the unmanned Surveyor crafts to the manned Apollo missions to the Moon, from the Mariner missions to Mars to the Voyager spacecraft—has opened up the entire Solar system to man.

However, what makes Ehricke unique is that, much like the great Classical composers,[3] he was at the same time a great visionary.

For example, in a 1966 paper on the subject of "Solar Transportation," he begins,

Let us leapfrog to the fall of the year 2000… By doing so, we will be able to describe the status of solar transportation in our time as well as to look back at the events of the past three and one-half decades which produced the advanced state of interplanetary travel which we enjoy at the turn of the millennium…. We have rendezvoused with, and planted an automatic scientific station on, the asteroid Icarus, which approaches the Sun as close as 0.169 AU, or about 47 percent of the distance of Mercury, and which swings out beyond the orbit of Mars to an aphelion distance of 1.68 AU. Our helionauts, as these men who fly our large interplanetary vehicles call themselves in this era of continuing specialization, have covered the solar system from the sun-scorched shores of Mercury to the icy cliffs of the Saturn moon Titan. They have crossed, and some have died doing so, the vast asteroid belt between Mars and Jupiter and have passed through the heads of comets. Owing to the pioneer spirit, the courage and the knowledge of our helionauts and of those engineers, scientists and technicians behind them, astrophysicists today work in a solar physics station on Mercury; biologists experiment on Mars, backed by a well supplied research and supply station on the Mars moon Phobos; planetologists have landed on Venus; and teams of scientists right now study what has turned out to be the two most fascinat-

ing planets of our solar system, Jupiter and Saturn, from research stations on Callisto and Titan.

As you know, we also have begun to utilize some of the discoveries. Our metal ore mining and processing facilities on Mercury are just three years old. On Mars, a long-range program has just been started to induce in the circumpolar regions of the northern and southern hemisphere, large scale cultures of special Mars-hardened plants, the result of twenty years of biological and agricultural research on Earth, on the Moon and on Mars proper. These plants are suitable for human consumption. While initially they will support the growing research base on Mars, it is expected that, within the next 50 years, Mars will export foodstuffs to Earth.

The traffic between Earth and Mercury, Earth and Mars, and Earth to Jupiter has become heavy enough to warrant the establishment of an orbital supply and rescue station at Venus. This station has worked successfully and has saved lives during the past eight years. Venus is a particularly useful place for a helionautical "coast guard" station, because this planet's orbital elements complement those of Earth for missions to Mercury as well as to Mars, Jupiter, and beyond.

In this rigorous play of the imagination, Ehricke invented a very real future for mankind.

A Collaboration of Visionary Geniuses

In 1981, Krafft Ehricke came into collaboration with Lyndon and Helga LaRouche, writing for *Fusion* magazine, speaking at conferences, and joining the advisory board of the Schiller Institute. It should be no surprise that LaRouche and Ehricke would find such an affinity of purpose, as both have spent the majority of their lives thinking about the progress of the human species *as a whole*, and both actively organized to make an upshift of the human species within the universe. LaRouche has done that with his life's work in economics, as a presidential candidate and statesman, and continues to do it to this day; Ehricke in his work outlining man's future in the Solar system.

Krafft Ehricke expressed the outlook which drove him very precisely in a 1957 work called "The Anthropology of Astronautics" in which he defined three fun-

---

3. In whom freedom of imagination and rigor of implementation were united. Johannes Brahms said, "Without craftsmanship, inspiration is a mere reed shaken in the wind." And Ludwig von Beethoven wrote at the top of his famous "Grosse Fuge," "As rigorous as it is free."

damental laws governing man's nature as a space-faring species:

First Law: Nobody and nothing under the natural laws of this universe impose any limitations on man except man himself.

Second Law: Not only the Earth, but the entire Solar System, and as much of the universe as he can reach under the laws of nature, are man's rightful field of activity.

Third Law: By expanding through the universe, man fulfills his destiny as an element of life, endowed with the power of reason and the wisdom of the moral law within himself.

These laws are philosophical laws, but they're not *only* philosophical; they correspond absolutely with Lyndon LaRouche's discoveries in the science of physical economy.

Developing the 'Seventh Continent'

For the last decade of his life, Ehricke focused his efforts on the development of the Moon, which he saw as the first crucial step in the *extraterrestrialization* of mankind. The primary question to be explored was (and is still today): How will man change and develop the Moon as an environment with unique characteristics, and *how will the Moon change and develop mankind?*

One illustrative example that Krafft himself brings up: On Earth, the biosphere came into existence first, and following that, mankind came along. On the Moon, however, it will be the reverse: man will arrive first, and only then it will be possible for life to exist there. How will this change our value judgments and our view of "nature"?

Krafft thought through rigorously and extensively how to establish the first permanent colony and industry on the Moon. Contemplate that for a moment: Not a short-term mission to land and leave again, or a temporary habitat; but a permanent, self-sustaining colony, where people's identity will be that of residents of the Moon, rather than Earth.

Painting by Chris Sloan

Krafft Ehricke invented the Lunar Slide Lander as an alternative to powered descent to the lunar surface, which would use 90% less propellant by taking advantage of the Moon's sandy and glassy soil to slow the vehicle.

Krafft said of the Moon, in a 1984 paper called "Lunar Industrialization and Settlement—Birth of Polyglobal Civilization": "It is a seventh continent, almost as large as the Americas. It is large enough to support a civilization. It alone offers the opportunity to create a strong exo-industrial economy based on highly advanced nuclear, cybernetic, and material processing technologies, ultimately turning large parts of the once-barren lunar surface into a lush oasis of life, capable eventually of exporting even foodstuffs to orbiting installations, if not to Earth."

Of the first lunar city, he said:

Selenopolis, city-state of lunar civilization and the lunar biosphere... [is a] network of enclosures, gradually expanding to cover many square miles of surface and subsurface.... It embodies urban, rural, agricultural, industrial and resort areas... each with a different Earth-like climate. Agricultural sections can be completely controlled to maximize productivity...

[Selenopolis and the selenosphere will be] a fully developed lunar world with a large population underwritten by industry. This stage is contingent upon a strong economic foundation, a very high degree of self-sufficiency, particularly in food production, and a powerful fusion energy base.

Lunar civilization must not be in a "receiver" position, vis-a-vis Earth. It must be economically self-determined, to a large extent. Much will depend on lunar political status and prospects by the end of Development Stage 4: will this be a colony of Earth, part of the common heritage of terrestrial mankind? Or will it be an independent political entity with Selenians in control of their own world? On a foundation of fusion power, the vast potential of the lunar economy renders the latter alternative possible and hence likely.

In order for man to accomplish this, Ehricke addressed several necessary categories of development:

1. Transportation
2. Energy
3. Resources and industry
4. Man's identity

He conceived of five stages of development, each of which depends upon the accomplishments of the previous stage. Early stages include prospecting for lunar resources; a complete and detailed lunar mapping; base site selection; experimentation with lunar materials (including automated labs on the lunar surface for oxygen extraction); and the establishment of a Circumlunar Space Station, with a Moon Ferry to transport workers between lunar orbit and the surface.

Later stages include a full-fledged mining and industrial operation, with a Central Lunar Processing Complex, supplied by automated feeder stations which mine at remote locations. Ehricke imagined the extensive potentials of lunar products:

Products will include sheet metal and trusses of aluminum, magnesium, titanium, iron, or alloys; castings, bars, wires, powders of pure or alloyed materials; glasses; glass wool; ceramics; refractories; fibrous and powdered ceramics; insulation; conductors; anodized metals; coatings, including almost perfectly reflective sodium coating (since sodium can be freely used on the Moon and in orbits, whereas on Earth it reacts with water and is dulled by oxidation); thin film materials; silicon chips; solar cells; entire structures of various metals and alloys for lunar and orbital installations (they do not have to be made weather resistant); compound and fibrous materials; heat shields and insulation materials, as well as radiation shielding materials for space stations; propellant containers; entire orbiting facilities, such as space station and factory modules and liquid lunar oxygen depots; large portions of cislunar and interplanetary spacecraft; and so on.

These later stages would also include advanced transportation options to and from orbit; advanced habitats for longer-duration stays on the surface; and fusion power plants to support the growing lunar civilization. The expansion of lunar industry to intermediate and finished products leads to a positive balance of trade, which sets up the possibility of a self-sustaining and growing Selenopolis.

The Adulthood of Mankind

The primary product of this kind of development, however, is the transformation of humanity itself to a higher level. As Krafft Ehricke recognized, fulfilling our extraterrestrial imperative as a species will necessitate leaving behind the infancy of man—wars, xenophobia, anti-technology outlooks, and geopolitics. Instead, mankind must mature into adulthood. This is what motivated him to join the Schiller Institute and its fight to create a new renaissance—he recognized that technological advancement was not enough. It is the soul and emotions which must be uplifted in order for our species to develop.

That is precisely the potential we have today, with the emerging new paradigm—the end of the "limits to growth" and the beginning of man's infinite progress.

Lyndon LaRouche expressed the mission before us in this way:

All mankind has a commitment, an innate commitment, to create knowledge of the future... All mankind must subdue their passions to conform to what the future of mankind represents. The point is the understanding of the individual to reach and achieve the ability of insight into what the future species must do: the improvement of the human species! Lifting the human species out of its ordinary existence, taking it out of its mediocrities.[4]

---

4. Sept. 13, 2016, in a private discussion with associates.

KRAFFT EHRICKE

The Moral Imperative of Space Exploration

by Marsha Freeman

By expanding through the Universe, man fulfills his destiny as an element of life, endowed with the power of reason and the wisdom of the moral law within himself.

—Krafft Ehricke

Krafft Ehricke was one of the most remarkable men of the Twentieth Century, whose work, more than 30 years after his death, embodies the moral imperative and provides the guideposts along the pathway to the future. Although his contributions to space exploration spanned the entire range of scientific and engineering concepts, from the utilization of Earth orbit, to the industrial development of the Moon, and exploration throughout the Universe—most of which, decades later, still remain to be realized—what distinguished him from other talented and creative visionaries was his uncompromising and passionate commitment to the future of mankind.

To Krafft Ehricke, space exploration was not simply an end in itself—no matter how important that practical end may be—but embodied the rekindling of the noblest qualities of humanity. The incorporation of man into the Universe would be a concrete expression of his creative potential, and that of the Universe, itself. In his view, the mastery of the universe would require that mankind recapture the morality as well as the creative

Krafft Ehricke
(1917-1984)

qualities that were under threat, and almost entirely destroyed, by the anti-human, anti-growth, and anti-science Malthusian disease of the 1960s. He was able to see that the logical consequence of this self-destructive pathway could be the very end of civilization. This gave great passion and urgency to his life's work, dedicated to make available to mankind the alternative "extraterrestrial imperative," to realize the great potential that lies within civilization, and just beyond the Earth. But in order to accomplish this evolution of man, mankind would have to marshal not only his science and technology, but "the moral law within himself."

One may wonder why Krafft Ehricke's name is not a household word in the history of spaceflight, like that of Wernher von Braun, who, in fact, lauded Krafft Ehricke's contributions to his own work. The reason is that Krafft Ehricke never bowed to popular opinion. He never changed or "toned down" his thinking in order to become acceptable to the ideological mores of the time. While his universal principles were recognized and greatly admired by his peers, with the zero growth cultural paradigm shift of the late 1960s, they had become "unpopular."

We came into contact with Krafft Ehricke after he had read the April 1981 issue of *Fusion* magazine, with a cover story on using fusion propulsion for colonizing

Krafft Ehricke at the 1955 annual congress of the International Astronautical Federation, Copenhagen.

ideas to make them more acceptable. This is the societal sickness that Krafft Ehricke passionately fought against his entire life.

To Krafft Ehricke, there was no compromise with principles or the sanctity of the human mind, which was a central characteristic of his philosophical outlook. When discussing how he mentally survived Nazi rule in Germany, in an interview, excerpted in a 1960 book by space historian Shirley Thomas, *Men of Space,* Krafft Ehricke said he always had the tendency to reserve ardent judgment on important things. I would go along only so far, then I just wouldn't be told. No matter what it was, what the field, I wanted to think it out for myself. This was instinctive at first; later I was consciously afraid to surrender my capability of judgement. With the change in government, the advent of Hitler in 1933, this trait protected me—though it also got me into great difficulty … it helped me very greatly in holding a line of thought in the Nazi era. … I like to paraphrase the saying 'My home is my castle.' To me, my mind is my castle. A part of it no one may enter. … I must have this ultimate, internal refuge, in which I am completely myself; only then am I really an individual.

space. He wrote a letter to the editor, stating that he had also developed concepts for using fusion energy in space. The editor invited him to contribute to the publication, which he happily did. Krafft Ehricke's concepts for the advanced fusion propulsion that could take man beyond the Moon, followed upon his development, in the 1960s, of the world's first energetic liquid hydrogen upper stage, which earned him the moniker, "father of the Centaur rocket." The Centaur opened up the entire Solar system for exploration by the robotic representations of man's intelligence.

While an Associate Editor of *Fusion*, I met Krafft Ehricke in October 1981 at his home in La Jolla, California. He showed me a file of letters from publishers, rejecting his manuscript for a 1971 book, titled, "The Extraterrestrial Imperative." The publishers objected that the book was "too optimistic," and promoted technologies such as nuclear energy, which were "unpopular." The book has never been published.

When the Fusion Energy Foundation and the Schiller Institute were organizing a Krafft Ehricke Memorial Conference in 1985, following his death in December the previous year, a German-born scientist at NASA who was asked to participate, declined, saying that Krafft Ehricke stubbornly would not change or adapt his

Today, due to the demoralization in much of the U.S. space community, despite stunning advancements, such as long-term living and working in space, exploring every major body in the Solar system, and increasingly uncovering the secrets of the universe, scientists have, in many cases, accepted limits on their vision for the future. Krafft Ehricke insisted that there are *no* limits on man, except those that he imposes on himself.

The Power of Reason

Krafft Ehricke never doubted that man would develop the technologies that would take him into space. But in 1957, even before the opening of the Space Age with the launch of Sputnik, he crafted what he considered to be most crucial—the philosophical worldview that should guide whatever progression of technologies would be developed to explore space. His three laws of astronautics were included in an article under a title curious for the usual writings about space policy: "The Anthropology of Astronautics" (see page 3, this issue).

Krafft Ehricke's 1957 "Three Fundamental Laws of Astronautics" state:

EAP

In November 1981, Krafft Ehricke, accompanied by his wife, Inge, joined Helga Zepp-LaRouche on a speaking tour in Germany. Here, he is speaking to the European Labor Party.

1. Nobody and nothing under the natural laws of this universe impose any limitations on man except man himself.
2. Not only the Earth, but the entire Solar system, and as much of the universe as he can reach under the laws of nature, are man's rightful field of activity.
3. By expanding through the Universe, man fulfills his destiny as an element of life, endowed with the power of reason and the wisdom of the moral law within himself.

The ultimate anthropological meaning of space flight, Krafft Ehricke says in the article, will be mankind's ability to "live elsewhere."

In 1970, when the zero growth counterculture was becoming hegemonic and Krafft Ehricke was preparing the manuscript for his book, *The Extraterrestrial Imperative,* he created a chart to make explicit why development, representing a Renaissance view of man, was imperative. The graphic depicting Growth Versus No Growth, makes starkly clear what the consequence of a philosophy of limits would be. While the choice of growth leads to an educated population, international cooperation, and advances in technology and science, the "No Growth" pathway leads to regional chauvinism, geopolitics, mass starvation, epidemics, and war. Look around the world before you, and you see the consequences of the "No Growth" path that Krafft Ehricke warned, more than 40 years ago, would result from a bestial view of mankind.

The depth of Krafft Ehricke's understanding that it was not technology, per se, that would enable man to create new civilizations beyond Earth, but a revolution in cultural, moral, and political values—those embodied in the European Renaissance, the German Classics, and the United States Constitution—found a coherence with those of the Schiller Institute, which was founded by Helga Zepp-LaRouche in 1984. Moreover, the Institute, and other organizations founded by Lyndon and Helga LaRouche, were engaged in a parallel fight to create a cultural and political paradigm shift, back to the Renaissance ideals that had created the New World.

The Institute was founded to promote a return to classical culture, scientific advance, and economic development, as the alternative to the destructive economic, geopolitical, and counterculture policies that were destroying the Western Alliance, and the future of mankind. Krafft Ehricke joined the Advisory Board of the Schiller Institute.

Helga Zepp-LaRouche described this coherence of ideas: Like herself, she said, Krafft Ehricke

was also convinced ... that only through space travel, only when man lifts his eyes from the Earth, looks into the stars and actually thinks what his role can be, can we achieve what Schiller called the dignity of man. And only if we start to think about space, and the colonization of space, will the Age of Reason that the great hu-

EIRNS

Upon return from his European trip, Krafft Ehricke related to this author his serious concern about the political situation he witnessed in Germany.

manists of European civilization were thinking of accomplishing, be possible. That was the belief of Schiller, that was the belief of Krafft Ehricke. The fact that man is capable of reason, even under the most horrible condition of crisis, is our most fundamental belief.

In November 1984, the Schiller Institute held its third international conference. Unable to attend due to illness, Krafft Ehricke sent the following message to the meeting, locating his prescription for the future of mankind in space, within the long sweep of history that should inform mankind's future path:

Greetings to the Friedrich Schiller Institute, to its Chairman, Helga Zepp-LaRouche; to its goal of a strong, revived American alliance with Europe, and to the defeat of the neo-Malthusian 'Green' parties menacing Western Europe.

I have been from the Moon to light years out and never found a limit to growth. ... Growth is the increase in knowledge, in wisdom, in the capacity for growing in new ways. Crises must be solved by leaping over the apparent limits to growth. ... At the present point in history, our highly technological civilization faces another crisis of energy, materials, production space, and means of material processing. But man's capacity for reason allows him to establish a "third earth" in the extraterrestrial environment

based on a more concentrated form of energy—nuclear fission and fusion. ... If four or five or six billion people will fall back on a lifestyle of a very embryonic mankind, it will destroy mankind by billions, and it will devastate the biosphere.

Civilization is the ascendancy beyond brutality, beyond the recognition of plurality, the recognition that there are various ways to live and in which to explore nature. ... Medieval European Civilization, frozen in the narrowness of its small, rigidly controlled communities and tightly bound to all-powerful religious dogmas, was in the Twelfth and Thirteenth Centuries dangerously close to becoming another static civilization, like those of ancient China, Japan, India, or the Incas on this continent. The sudden recognition that here there was the wide and beautiful Earth waiting to be taken by man, overwhelmed and emboldened the great thinkers of that time. ... This was the crowning achievement of the Renaissance.

Now we begin to realize that the Solar system, and probably even parts of this Galaxy, can be ours. The consequences, for all phases of human existence, of the practical application of the second law of astronautics, during the coming centuries, almost defy our imagination, just as the world of today would be almost inconceivable to the Renaissance pioneers. We today are merely the shipbuilders for the men and women who will enter a new era of discoveries and lay the foundations for those who will come after them, those who will develop planetary technologies and create cosmic civilizations.

Krafft Ehricke's assertion that "civilization is the ascendancy beyond brutality," was under existential threat, no different than that under fascism in the 1930s. On Nov. 28, 1981 Krafft Ehricke gave a presentation in New York City, having just returned from a speaking tour in Europe with Helga Zepp-LaRouche.

Riding in the car from the airport in New York to Manhattan, Krafft Ehricke was clearly shaken by his encounter with violent anti-nuclear Green mobs at speaking venues in Germany. He opened his presentation on the extraterrestrial imperative, stating: "It is a little bit disconcerting that the same shock troop kind of tactics stand at the end of one's life as I have seen as a young man in Berlin in [19]29, '30, '31." He continued, "The youth of West Germany and other nations have unfortunately been greatly misled ... today, if a person even talks about space flight or nuclear energy, then the 'ecopaths,' the cultural pessimists, and associated professional chaoticists literally characterize this to be an outright provocation that they will do their utmost to prevent." The police had to be called to prevent violence when students at a university venue tried to bar the speaker's entry.

EIRNS/Stuart Lewis

Krafft Ehricke was very disturbed, he reported in a presentation in New York City in November 1981, that he had encountered Green "mobs" at German universities, opposed to his program for nuclear energy and space exploration.

The Greens have no positive proposals, Krafft Ehricke said. But assume that it is true, that there are limits to growth, and the "technological clock had to be turned back to more primitive times, in order to 'save' the planet." What are the consequences? To what agony do we condemn a majority of mankind? What is our moral imperative? To Krafft Ehricke, the answers to these questions were not academic, but would test the "moral law" within mankind.

Let's for the sake of argument assume that their view [of limits to growth] is correct. Are we thus to suffer indefinitely, because relief-providing technology could be misused? In 1979, of all things, in the Year of the Child of the United Nations, there were 12 million children who did not reach their first birthday. That's 50 percent more than all battle deaths in World War I, in four years. And that is an outrage to a species that calls itself civilized. This is to say nothing of the suffering of those children before they died, to say nothing of the suffering of the mothers who

bore those children, just to see them die and not be able to feed them—to hear them cry day and night. This is unbelievable agony.

But there is an alternative; that of the "open world," where science and technology create the growth that allows mankind to leave the Earth entirely, and create new worlds, where he is not limited to one, original home planet. This can only come about, he insisted, if the "moral law within him" is the driving force of the future.

Earlier that year, in a letter to the new Fortieth President of the United States, Ronald Reagan, on March 3, 1981, Krafft Ehricke described dramatically the moral crisis faced by mankind. While he naturally outlined his concepts for the steps the President should take in space exploration, he located them not in an academic or even scientific argument, but minced no words in placing them in the context of what gave them great urgency.

Space, he said, "will not turn this planet into a paradise, but will help to combat a much more important problem—to prevent it from becoming a hell. ... Indeed, Earth becomes an evermore unpleasant 'space ship' at an increasing rate for an increasing part of its population. Rising poverty, wrong economic and social agendas, wrong energy policies ... and spreading political intolerance causing immeasurable suffering to millions of refugees in Africa and Southeast Asia, as well as Central America—these inhuman realities are with us, not because of what technology and industry do, but because of what they are prevented from doing."

Referencing his extraterrestrial imperative, Krafft Ehricke outlines for the new President the manned missions, lunar development, space applications, and series of robotic Solar system missions that should be the center of his space policy.

He concludes on this philosophical note:

The history of flight is a history of overcoming limits to growth through human courage and engineering creativity, through [a] thirst for freedom and a commitment to infinity. It has led us into the extraterrestrium with countless challenges to our courage, resolve and creativity—forward-oriented, solution-oriented and, finally, free from the recriminations of past history, if we can humanly rise to this challenge.

Living in the Future

Six weeks before his death, and while gravely ill, Krafft Ehricke traveled from his home in California to Washington, D.C., and delivered the keynote address at the "Lunar Bases and Space Technology of the 21st Century" conference, held October 29-31, 1984, sponsored by NASA and hosted by the National Academy of Sciences. The organizers of the conference—lunar scientists from NASA's Johnson Space Center in Houston—had recently become familiar with Krafft Ehricke's work through a series of articles he had written for *Fusion* magazine, which I had given them at an earlier lunar conference in Houston. Wendell Mendell, the moderator of the Washington conference, had never met Krafft Ehricke before this event, but easily recognized the unique quality of the speaker.

Mendell, in introducing the keynote, said there were a number of colleagues and friends who had asked to make preliminary remarks. One was Fred Durant III, a man with a stunning career himself, as a World War II Navy flight instructor, president of the American Rocket Society, president of the International Astronautical Federation (IAF), and top official at the National Air & Space Museum, from 1964 to 1980. He died one year ago, at the age of 98. Fred Durant met Krafft Ehricke in the early 1950s, and related how, in 1952, he presented a paper for Krafft at the third IAF Congress.

After reviewing some of what Krafft Ehricke had accomplished, he observed:

> But Krafft is not happy unless he is writing of what *can* be done, and what our progeny, what our grandchildren may see. I will say that it is a lonely world where Krafft lives part of the time, because it is the future. ...

Krafft Ehricke began to live in the future in a movie theater at the age of 12, after watching "The Woman in the Moon." His mentor, Hermann Oberth, had been the

EXPEDITION ARES
A Saga from the Dawn of Interplanetary Travel

INTRODUCTION
Krafft Ehricke's Manned Mission to Mars

When he began writing *Expedition Ares* in 1948, German-born space scientist Krafft Ehricke (1917-1984) had been in the United States for one year, and was living on the U.S. Army base at Ft. Bliss, Texas. He was one of the German space pioneers helping to transfer to the U.S. Army the rocket technology which the Germans had developed before and during the World War II, and had brought with them to the United States. Dr. Ehricke was writing up, from memory, the technical details of the V-2, or A-4 rocket, and helping to translate the reports of other members of the group into English.

Most of the men were learning English, many by sharing the one available dictionary, and watching cowboy movies. Krafft Ehricke applied his engineering knowledge and engaged his imagination to look toward the future; he created a story, written in English, describing the first manned missions to Mars.

At that time, the only large liquid-fueled rockets ever launched were the wartime V-2s, which just barely reached space. But Ehricke could see a time, even if far off in the future, when the finicky technology of chemically propelled rockets would be mastered, the political will would be marshalled, and the resources committed, so that man would

Space visionary Krafft Ehricke (left) was interviewed by CBS correspondent Walter Cronkite on Sept. 26, 1966. Ehricke, who worked for North American Rockwell at the time, is discussing the features of a reusable transport vehicle that he designed. The initial stage of the vehicle consists of 12 turbo-ramjet engines. A supersonic ramjet engine allows the vehicle to achieve orbital velocity; the hypersonic spaceplane atop the transport would return to a landing site for reuse.

Courtesy of Krafft Ehricke

embrace the possibility of leaving the Earth, to head for the stars.

Ehricke chose a writing style brilliantly employed by a 19th Century predecessor—Jules Verne—who had fired the imagination of youth all over Europe, through his series of engaging books about an imaginary trip to the Moon. Using the development of a delightful array of characters, Verne had summarized for his readers the scientific knowledge of his time about space travel, and Luna.

Expedition Ares

Ehricke's setting is more than 400 years in the future, when space travel throughout the Solar System is commonplace,

21st CENTURY   Spring 2003   29

21st Century Science & Technology

Krafft Ehricke always resided in the future. In 1948, in the United States for only one year, he penned "Expedition Ares: A Saga from the Dawn of Interplanetary Travel." The story looks "back" at the first manned expedition to Mars in the year 2000 from 400 years in the future.

technical adviser for the film, and had created a model Moon rocket that was put on display.

In 1934, when he was 17 years old, Krafft Ehricke wrote a manuscript that included several short stories, titled, "Thoughts of Space and Man." The first piece describes how every 50 (!) years, scientists from around the world and every scientific discipline would meet to discuss the current breakthroughs in science.

Looking about six decades into the future, as a young man, Krafft Ehricke wrote a short story, simply titled, "To My Loving Mother with Thanks." According to his family, Krafft Ehricke's mother "moved heaven and earth to feed his dreams, as a youth, finding scientific books from around the world that he could start with, and then advance with his own knowledge."

But beside learning from his own, independent study, Krafft Ehricke also had to cope with school. His family relates that "as a youth, he was having problems

With lunar industrialization well underway, Astropolis would be built—a virtual city-state in Earth orbit. Far from today's concept of a "space station," Astropolis would be a trading post between the economic activities of the Earth and Moon, and a training facility for travel through the Solar system.

gineers, dreamers and adventurers, found themselves on the brink of vast emptiness beyond which new worlds lured and stimulated their desire to remove the barriers erected between man and star. The first attempt to realize these dreams is known in history as "Expedition Ares." Later missions, in his story, would take crewed ships to every planet in the Solar system.

The vehicles, and propulsion system, the necessary in-space maintenance and repair of the ship, the dangers through the Asteroid Belt and encounter with a previously unknown asteroid, are told in great detail. Many of the challenges, and failures, faced on these missions would happen in real life, throughout what would later become the first 60 years of the Space Age.

But exploring and utilizing near-Earth space, industrializing the Moon, and exploring our neighboring planets was not a limit for Krafft Ehricke. His vision of moving off the Earth started with a space "station," but not what we have come to know through the International Space Station. Krafft Ehricke's station would be an orbiting city, with thousands of inhabito

with math. His teachers were frustrated," so his mother "got him one tutor after another. Finally, one of the tutors told her there was nothing wrong with his ability to understand the math, but that he was so far advanced, they could not follow his work, nor understand it." But in one case, "that particular tutor kept working with him because he was interested in the mathematics he was doing, and he was learning from his student."

The short story dedicated to his mother recounts the expedition of one Captain Knuth Ehrich, who, in 1991, began a manned voyage to Venus. The trip was "made possible through the new Ehrich atomic ion rocket." The expedition "would look for new settlement areas for mankind, and conduct scientific research." The captain had a crew of 30, representing the various fields of the natural sciences, and proceeded "by way of the Moon." The commissioning body for the expedition was the "International Governance Conference" in New York, with the participation of 48 nations.

In 1948, one year after arriving in the United States, Krafft Ehricke wrote (in English), "Expedition Ares: A Saga from the Dawn of Interplanetary Travel." Set more than 400 years in the future, the story looks "back" at the history of space exploration and at Expedition Ares, a manned mission to Mars in the year 2000. At the turn into the Twenty-first Century, Krafft Ehricke writes, "circling Earth in small scout rockets, scientists and en-

The goal of space exploration, Krafft Ehricke believed, was to cut the cord to Earth and free mankind to explore the cosmos, creating scientific breakthroughs and establishing new civilizations. Androcells would be independent, new man-made planets, able to freely roam the Solar system, where the new society, and no longer the Earth, was considered "home."

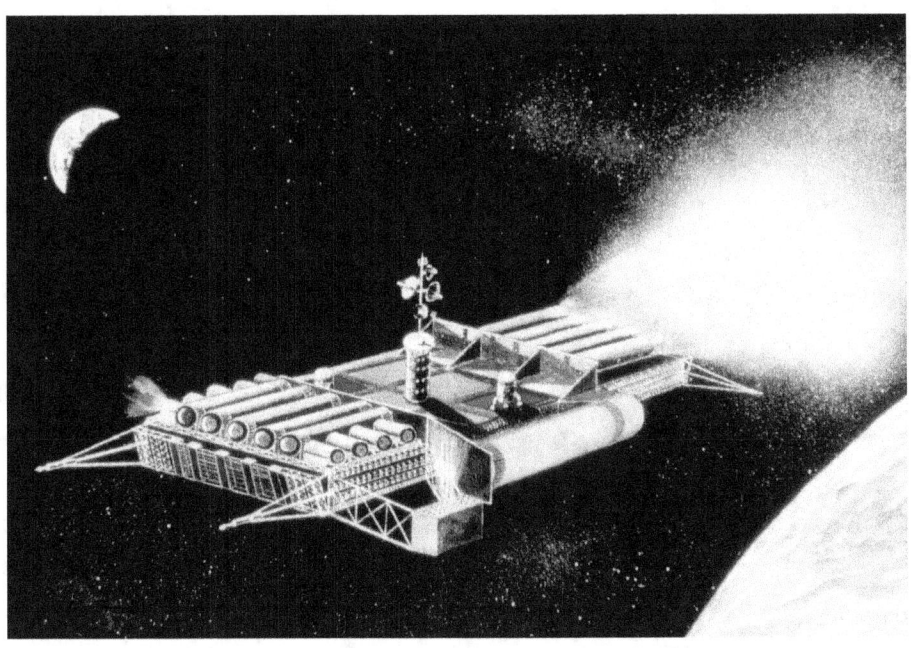

The first step in "extraterrestrialization," is the establishment of scientific and economic activities on the Moon. In this painting by Krafft Ehricke, a nuclear-powered freighter is bringing products from the Moon to Earth orbit, and will bring needed materials from Earth, to the Moon.

ants. In addition to living quarters and all necessary complements for crew, it would include facilities such as an orbital hospital for those who would benefit from microgravity for treatment and recuperation, facilities for tourists, a university, farms, and recreation. Krafft Ehricke called this city in orbit, "Astropolis," an urban facility, to be the first step in "extraterrestrialization."

His lunar industrialization program, expanded over the 1970s, became an elegantly detailed engineering blueprint, motivated by his concept of the Extraterrestrial Imperative, as his proposed follow-on to the Apollo missions. A five-stage program culminates in the completion of his city on the Moon, Selenopolis; not a base, not a habitat, but a city with thousands of citizens, who create a new civilization, economically, politically and sociologically independent from the Earth.

"A new branch of psychology, exopsychology, and of sociology, exosociology, will evolve," he wrote, as "the transition beyond Earth is very profound."

With that existing infrastructure, with the resources from the Moon, such as helium-3 for fusion power plants, mankind would be ready to move civilization out into deep space.

The penultimate freedom for mankind would be to create a "new Earth." Not only cities on the existing planets in our Solar system, but autonomous cities in space, with propulsion systems that would take this new Earth into deep space. These "androcells" would not return to Earth, but as self-sufficient societies, would be free to travel the Solar system. Krafft Ehricke referred to androcells as "man-made planetellas," which are "mobile, and seek other resources, beyond the Earth-Moon system." Finally, man would have cut the umbilical cord to Earth.

The civilization of these "roaming, self-sufficient worlds," he explained, "is truly three-dimensional. ... [They] can circle our Sun in independent orbits." It is a "politically independent city-state, trading with the Earth, Moon, orbiting manufacturing facilities, and other places, forming new cultural cells of a mankind whose choice of living in space has increased tremendously, thereby adding to the plurality of human civilization."

Krafft Ehricke could imagine future pioneers off to explore and develop the entire Solar system, much the way explorers during the first Age of Exploration created a new civilization in the New World.

He also outlined, in an interview in 1970, his view that by going into space, man had created a three-dimensional civilization, but that adding time into the concept made it four dimensional. Interstellar flight, he proposes, "particularly to stellar migration and interstellar or galactic nomadism, are the theater of action on which civilization will grow into four-dimensional (space-time) proportions," he explained. While this may seem fantastic, he assures us that, "Travel beyond our Solar system, to distant stars, sounds as unreal today as a manned landing on the Moon must have seemed just a generation or two ago."

The Moon

Krafft Ehricke was well known for saying:

Some people used to say, "If God had wanted man to fly, he would have given him wings." Now we can say, "If God had wanted man to

Selenopolis, as envisioned by Krafft Ehricke and depicted in this painting by Christopher Sloan, is not a habitat or lunar "base," but a city on the Moon. Powered by fusion tokamak reactors, the development of "Earth's seventh continent" would be the stepping stone to mankind's expeditions on the "ocean" of space.

become a spacefaring species, he would have given man a Moon."

For Krafft Ehricke, the first step in the true extraterrestrialization of space would be the industrial development of the Moon.

At the time of his death, Krafft Ehricke had completed a book, the culmination of more than a decade of intensive research, titled, *The Seventh Continent: The Industrialization and Settlement of the Moon,* which has yet to be published.

He described the Moon "as the prime model of developing a new world at the outset of androspheric expansion, for several reasons. The Moon is our partner in this double-planet system only 2.5 to 3 flight-days away, less time than it takes an oil tanker to get from the Persian Gulf to New England. The Moon is a potential source of raw materials and a suitable place for materials processing and for establishing the first extraterrestrial biosphere. Its surface area almost equals the area of the Americas, which lends it enough gravity for human comfort and plant growth." The Moon, he also said, will offer us "a new world of great beauty."

Selenians "can trek through the lunar world into the mountains, to the picturesque 'coastlines' of the *mare*, the wilderness ranges at the poles. ... When the Sun sets, Earth stands out as a crescent in the sky of the Moon's near side. The slowly waxing mother planet bathes the moonscape in mild light of rising intensity."

"The Selenians live truly on the shores of the interplanetary ocean. They will travel with ease between the one-sixth 'g' surface gravity [of the Moon], and the weightlessness of their circumlunar outposts, and later between their world and those of Mars, asteroids, and the moons of Jupiter and Saturn. The Selenians indeed live in a cosmically Open World."

By the middle of the next century, he said, "I see a polyglobal three-dimensional civilization. In retrospect, its foundations were laid in the twilight of the past millennium, by those who understood the magnificent call of the extraterrestrial imperative. ... But there were those among them who did not have the capacity for understanding that their world reaches to the stars; and so they rooted and burrowed into the ground. They regressed, whining and shouting slogans. Fearful to grow, they atrophied to barren stumps on a clump of earth and became still births of the biosphere. ... In a miserable world of stagnation, poverty, and backwardness, they may indeed manage to trigger the ultimate catastrophe of releasing nuclear energy in an entropic holocaust."

But this was not preordained. Instead, "the new humanity, Homo sapiens extraterrestris ... will set sail on a new course into the Open World of limitless growth—negentropically, and steady as you go!"

As his family will attest, Krafft Ehricke applied great intensity and concentration to his work. He was driven by a passion to enable the real potential for creative discovery, to apply science and technology to end the degradation of a great portion of the world's people, and to demonstrate that our most noble aspirations would be fulfilled by the civilizations we would create off the Earth.

First published in the German-language magazine FUSION, Vol. 37, No. 2, 2016.

Classical Music as Revolutionary Ideas, Not Entertainment

The following is an edited transcript of a report given by John Sigerson, the Schiller Institute Music Director, on a class given by him in Manhattan on March 11, 2017. A video of the full class, titled "Motivführung 101: Introduction to the Haydn-Mozart Revolution" is available here.

John Sigerson: This is the first of two classes. In terms of the content, I wanted to find a way of introducing to many people who really have no musical background whatsoever the three major breakthroughs, conceptual breakthroughs, scientific breakthroughs, in the musical domain:

One, the Florentine *bel canto* discovery around the period of Nicholas of Cusa.

Second, Bach's earthshaking discovery of the well-tempered domain of musical development, and

Third, the Haydn-Mozart revolution of *Motivführung*, with great attribution to Norbert Brainin, pointing that out and working with Lyn on that.

I started out with a presentation of a way of getting into that. I used the *cupola* of the *Santa Maria del Fiore* cathedral in Florence, and pointed out that, first of all, the incredible optimism that occurred even before Brunelleschi began to work on that, namely the de-

it.wikipedia.org/User:sailko

The dome of Florence's Santa Maria del Fiore.

Ricardo André Frantz

Filippo Brunelleschi's design for the dome used the principle of the catenary, to surmount the challenge of spanning the vast interior space of the cathedral.

cision in 1367 by the Florentines, especially the main architect there, whose name is Neri di Fioravante, who also rebuilt the *Ponte Vecchio*, and he lived through the black death of that period. In 1367 he, along with the rest of the Florentines who were working on the cathedral, which had been begun in 1294, decided that they wanted to create something which *does not use flying buttresses*, because they considered the flying buttresses as being outdated and ugly, because it was something that was external to the idea of a perfectly balanced, beautiful church. And it was that idea of rejecting the idea of flying buttresses—and I showed a picture of those—that was the leap that allowed them to build this huge octagonal space, which they had no idea how they were going to bridge, but they knew that it had to be done according to *new physical principles*, exactly the same idea that Lyn developed in the SDI effort.

Then I pointed out the incredible breakthrough of Brunelleschi in using the non-mathematical curve in the construction of the Cathedral, not just one curve, but the entire structure is based on this idea of this non-mathematical curvature, and that this is the way that the entire building is harmonically organized, but not according to whole number ratios, but according to a curvature which could not possibly even be described by whole number ratios. At that point I presented the *Nuper rosarum flores* motet that was composed by Guillaume Dufay for the March 25, 1436 consecration of the Cathedral. And I played that for people, and I pointed out that, really, Dufay's work was nowhere near being able to grasp the full implications of what Brunelleschi had accomplished, because of the fact that he was still stuck in the idea of the *cantus firmus*, which was very similar to the flying buttresses idea, an external support for musical development which was not actually integrated with the entire musical development.

EIRNS

Norbert Brainin (left), former primarius of the legendary Amadeus Quartet, gives a master class with young musicians in Dolna Krupa, Slovakia, Sept. 20-22, 1995.

I used that as a way of getting into the period of struggle to actually have a way of composing which is fully in harmony with Brunelleschi's breakthroughs. I won't go through everything here, but I presented an experiment which was done by Orlando di Lasso, which was published in 1600, called the *Prophetiae Sibyllarum*, which is an experimental piece, where he is trying to develop the musical system by attempting to work on a system of modulation. But it's not really completely successful. And then I jumped; I mentioned John Bull and his work on fugues, and then skipped to J.S. Bach, very quickly, and I played for people the air from his *Orchestral Suite No. 3* performed by Wilhelm Furtwängler, where I showed that especially the bass line of that— I don't know if you're familiar with that one, but it's this beautiful air, which has this beautiful walking bass in the bottom, and I pointed out that even the bass line could not have been composed without the development of the well-tempered system.

I was throwing a lot of things at a lot of people: I'm sure a lot of it went above people's heads, but I wanted to play for people a lot of different examples to show this, and I think some people did get it.

Let me run through the other examples, and I think you can figure out what I'm doing. I played a very short bit of Norbert Brainin's presentation on *Motivführung* at Dolna Krupa, at the famous Dolna Krupa seminars, where he points out that the only person who ever understood and resonated with this idea of *Motivführung* was you, Lyn. And then I played the two different Haydn pieces, one the String Quartet Opus 20, No. 2, which is before Haydn's breakthrough on *Motivführung*, and then a little bit of the Opus 33, No. 3, which shows this idea. And that made really quite clear, even with small amounts, the nature of Haydn's breakthrough with *Motivführung* that way. Then I followed that up playing a little bit of Mozart's "Dissonant" string quartet, and then moved to Mozart's motet *Ave verum corpus*, a little bit of discussion of that, and then counterposed that with *Heiliger Dankgesang* in Beethoven's Opus 132 string quartet, again playing little bits and then at the end a little bit of the Schubert Ninth Symphony, just pointing out the opening and counterposing Furtwängler's incredible performance of that with a not very incredible performance of that by John Eliot Gardiner.

That's the summary of it. Because we were doing this in the hotel room, I couldn't have any live music— the acoustics are terrible, there's no piano, so I relied solely on these examples, but next week we are going to hold it in a place where we can have some live examples, live demonstrations, and also go further into Florentine *bel canto* and to the questions of the well tempered tuning. So we'll get into the C=256 question, which I broached, but didn't get into in much detail.

LaRouche: That is good!

II. What Is Grand Strategy?

Germany Must Jump Aboard The New Silk Road Express!

by Helga Zepp-LaRouche, chairwoman of the German political party, Civil Rights Movement Solidarity (BüSo)

March 18—The atmosphere could hardly have been more uneasy between German Chancellor Angela Merkel und U.S. President Donald Trump during her visit to the White House. No handshake for the cameras, next to no eye contact, strained faces for both of them. Not only is there no chemistry between them, but it is obvious that in the current trans-Atlantic geometry, no solution for the tensions can be found. There is nonetheless a way out in sight, but it can only be found on a totally different, higher level—the win-win cooperation with China and the New Silk Road, which the United States and Germany have both been invited to join.

Given that Trump's election meant the defeat of the neoliberal, neoconservative policy of Hillary Clinton, whom he called "America's Angela Merkel," and that Merkel was considered "Obama's closest ally," it was not to be expected that the two of them would be on the same wavelength. Thus the *New York Times* headlined its coverage, "Merkel Meets Trump—The Defender Versus the Disrupter." When, during their joint press conference, a correspondent of *Die Welt* attempted to provoke Trump by bringing up the charge that British intelligence agency GCHQ had wiretapped him for the Obama Administration, Trump turned to Merkel and jokingly remarked, "At least we have something in common." Trump got the laughs for that, while Mrs. Merkel could barely muster a smile.

Similar unresolvable divergences were evident among the G20 finance ministers at their meeting in Baden-Baden, where they could not agree on formulations about "protectionism" and "fair trade" for a final communiqué.

The Chinese Solution

Much more promising, however, is the dynamic of China's comprehensive diplomatic initiatives in preparation for the May 14-15 summit, the Belt and Road Forum, in Beijing. Already more than 20 heads of state, 100 ministerial delegations, 150 leaders of major organizations, and 1,200 delegations of scientists, industry executives, and economists have confirmed their participation. Chinese State Councilor Yang Jiechi, who is responsible for preparing and coordinating the conference, visited President Trump and members of the Trump team in Washington at the end of February. Shortly thereafter, Trump invited President Xi Jinping for a two-day working summit, which is now tentatively set for some time in April at Mar-a-Lago, Trump's Florida estate. In contrast to Japanese Prime Minister Abe's visit to Trump's estate, the visit with the Chinese President is not expected to be about golf, but about comprehensive American-Chinese cooperation on economic and strategic questions.

At a press conference March 10 on the sidelines of the National People's Congress in Beijing, Yang Jiechi stressed to *China Daily* that the goal of the May 14-15 summit is to consolidate a "broad international consensus on the 'Belt and Road Initiative.' " This initiative was China's idea, but it will not be a solo performance by China, he said; a better analogy would be a symphony, he explained, performed by an orchestra composed of all participating countries.

Without a doubt, one of the most important strategic developments is that the President of the UN General Assembly, Peter Thomson, and the new UN Secretary General, Antonio Guterres, have announced that the UN will cooperate fully with China's New Silk Road initiative. Thomson stressed that Xi Jinping's vision "is the only future for mankind on this planet" in an interview with Xinhua. After Xi's keynote speech at the UN Palace of Nations in Geneva on Jan. 18, "Thomson and UN Secretary-General Antonio Guterres both pledged that the United Nations will join China in promoting world peace and development, and in realizing the goal of building a community of shared future for mankind," according to Xinhua Jan. 29.

That is not only definitely true, but China's conception of the New Silk Road has developed over the last three-and-a-half years into a unique strategic initiative going far beyond the original dimensions of the ancient Silk Road, and has become a development strategy for all the world's continents.

No one can contest that the several hundred New Silk Road projects—in different stages of realization—are approaching at a tremendous tempo the conception that *EIR* proposed in 2014 in a 370-page comprehensive study, *The New Silk Road Becomes the World Land-Bridge*. In other words, China and more than 70 other nations have now received the official support of the United Nations to make the longstanding dream of the Non-Aligned Movement for a new, just world economic order come true. And with that, it is also undeniable that it is the ideas and principles that Lyndon LaRouche has fought for, for more than fifty years, that are becoming dominant on the international plane, as Tunisian diplomat Dr. Ahmed Kedidi recently described in a remarkable article in the Qatari newspaper *Al-Sharq*.

Overcoming the Obstacles

Of course there are significant and even existential threats standing in the way of this vision of a united mankind, a vision which previously was conceived only by philosophers such as Confucius, Sri Aurobindo, Nicholas of Cusa, and Leibniz. Pressing instances include the extremely dangerous conflict over the North Korean missile tests (in reaction to the stationing of the THAAD missile defense system in South Korea and the U.S.-South Korean military maneuvers); the only partially mitigated crises in the Middle East; and the conflict escalating once again in Ukraine. Pragmatists and cultural pessimists will of course cite these crises, using Aristotelian arguments, as proof that the goal of a common future for mankind is an unattainable utopia.

But exactly the opposite mode of thinking is required. If we define the common interests of mankind from the standpoint of the future—of a vision of where we intend mankind to be in 10, 100, or 1,000 years—then we can imagine a higher level of reason, on which conflicts on a lower level are resolved. China's initiative for a New Silk Road—in which all countries can participate in win-win cooperation—proceeds precisely from this approach.

It will very soon be clear that President Trump can only realize his promise to rebuild U.S. infrastructure if countries with great expertise in this area, such as China, Japan, and Germany, participate in the process. In the same way, it is already clear that the further disintegration of Europe can only be stopped if European nations, along with China, decide to build up the Balkans and Southern Europe as part of the expansion of the New Silk Road. The conflict on the Korean peninsula is only solvable if North and South Korea return to a common strategy for development, which had been ended, under pressure from the Obama Administration, by the recently impeached President of South Korea, Park Geun-hye. This is only conceivable if the two Koreas are embedded in the dynamic of the new Silk Road.

And Europe could perhaps again evoke a western community of values, if it gave up its unspeakable attempts to make horrific deals to organize reception camps for refugees—which have become detention camps—and instead participated in a workable development strategy for Southwest Asia and Africa. But this presupposes that the representatives of the arrogant, neoliberal, trans-Atlantic Establishment come down off their high horses—or are replaced by other political forces.

This might appear unrealistic to many people today, but the moment in universal history has come, in which the best ideas that mankind's greatest thinkers have brought forward, must be put into practice. One of the most important conceptions of this kind is the method of thinking that Nicholas of Cusa developed with his *coincidentia oppositorum*, the coincidence of opposites. Nicholas fully realized—and he wrote of it—that what he was thinking had never been conceived by anyone else. But with this scientific method, he not only laid the basis for the Treaty of Westphalia, but also for the creation of new discoveries in science and Classical art.

If we are to solve the problems of mankind today, we have to start from Cusa's approach, an approach much like that of Confucianism, on which Chinese President Xi Jinping's vision is based. To better understand this approach, Cusa's *De Docta Ignorantia* and his associated memorandum in its defense are highly recommended readings.

INTERVIEW WITH NOMI PRINS

The Coming Banking Panic

Paul Gallagher interviewed financial expert Nomi Prins on March 16. See https://www.youtube.com/watch?v=kqQqsvRhtFc Edited excerpts follow.

Paul Gallagher: Hello. This is Paul Gallagher with LaRouche PAC television (https://larouchepac.com/). I'm co-editor of economics for *EIR*, and today I'm talking to Nomi Prins, who was for years—I think more than a decade—in investment banking with Goldman Sachs, Chase, and Lehman, as an analyst and also as a manager. She has been a very widely published analyst and expert on the banking system and banking history, and has published both as a speaker, and also in leading newspapers in the country. She has also written, if I'm not mistaken, something like nine books.

Former investment banker and author Nomi Prins.

Nomi Prins: Only seven.

Gallagher: Seven books on the subject, including the award-winning *Other People's Money* in 2004, the most recent one, *All the President's Bankers*, and the forthcoming *Partisans of Money*, about the history of the central bankers. She is also in the middle of a number of meetings with offices of the Congress right now.

So let me start, Nomi, by asking you: You've written an analysis piece on 2017, and what you expect for this year, in which you say that the stock and bond markets in the United States may crumble by the end of the year; that there will be a large upsurge in corporate defaults—and I think you give the figure that there already was quite an upsurge in 2016, in the European banks and the major losses that some of those banks have been reporting. Do you think that these events threaten another bank panic, like 2008?

Prins: I think that because the 2008 crisis, or bank panic, has not really been resolved, what has happened is that it's been shifted forward. And by that I mean, when we had the crisis in 2008, and we had all the interdependencies between the largest banks—not just in the United States, though prevalently in the United States, but then throughout the world—the solution to that was for the Federal Reserve to cut rates to zero, and launch a quantitative easing program, and to basically expand that program, not just in the United States to help liquidity and credit flow, but throughout the world.

So there's been an almost decade-long coordinated period of elevating the markets, and helping banks maintain liquidity, and keeping reserves from these banks that don't then get loaned into the main economy, or at least the lower echelons of the individual citizens, or smaller businesses of that main economy. And that's really what's been happening for almost a decade. So, at some point, there will be a "give" in that strategy. We've already had the Federal Reserve raise rates now by 75 basis points, beginning in December 2015 through March 2017, so effectively 25 basis points [one quarter of one percent] per year—which

isn't a very big number. But what that is doing, while other central banks are keeping rates at either negative or close to zero—so still keeping the equilibrium of zero-cost money throughout the world—is that it's hedging the possibility of more defaults to creep into the system.

So, on the one hand, the reaction of markets to all this cheap money, is to go up. There's nowhere else for money to go. Bonds are not returning any real interest, and high-grade bonds certainly aren't, so money has been pushed into the stock market, and it's kind of had a self-fulfilling bubble quality to it. But when these rates start going up, all the debt that's been created during this period starts to have to repay at potentially higher levels than it expected to repay. And so all the corporate debt that's been issued, all the money that's flowed throughout the world, all of a sudden has to consider retracting.

We've already started to see that since the 2015 hike in the Fed rates, which is that we had higher default rates in corporates, and also in U.S.-dollar denominated corporates throughout the world, than we've had in any of the years since the crisis started. And then we had a second bout of that in 2016. So we have the defaults in the corporate world increasing, almost in tandem with rates being raised. And so at some point that's going to create a situation where those companies start to have difficulties repaying, particularly in emerging markets outside the United States—that's going to hurt their markets. When those markets start going down, it starts to hurt the main markets. It starts to hurt the U.S. market, because it comes back, because confidence and credit starts to crumble throughout the world. It might start peripheral to the United States, but then it comes back to the United States.

And the same thing with Europe. There's a lot of volatility in the European markets—even though their stock markets have been doing very well, because the policy of the European Central Bank has been to keep rates at negative, and to continue to buy securities, and to basically flush the system with money. If that starts to become more expensive, then you will start to have corporate defaults increase more in Europe.

So we're really set up in a way, at a much more dangerous point than we were before the financial crisis of 2008, because now the world is sitting on a tremendously larger amount of debt. Right now, debt to GDP in the world is about three times—there's $325 trillion of debt relative to [perhaps $100 trillion of] GDP. It was less than one time debt to GDP before the financial crisis started. So, it's elevated quite a lot throughout the world.

Leverage Has Tripled

Gallagher: It went from one to one, to three to one?

Prins: Three to one. Basically the ratio since before the crisis, to after the crisis, has almost tripled. And we see that in the United States, it's gone from—it's over 100% now, or close to 100%, of debt to GDP, and that's not unique to the United States. Of course, in countries like Greece, it's 160% or 170%. This has all taken place because debt has been cheap to issue. When debt becomes more expensive to issue, and you have to repay debt that has been issued at a higher amount, but you don't have real growth to compensate for that, you don't have real profit to compensate for that—that's when markets start to get wobbly; that's when credit starts to tighten again. And that's when this entire quantitative easing—this central bank-coordinated process of keeping the money so cheap

BUSINESS

EXPRESS

US Economy 2017: Is Another Financial Crisis On the Way? European Banks Warn Against Easing Banking Regulations

European banking officials Monday warned against easing U.S. banking regulations, ... in currency manip...

lead ... ... sugo ...

CNN Money

The last thing Europe needs: another Greek crisis

EU set for CATASTROPHIC 2017: Fresh European banki crisis IMMINENT, top analy warns

ITALY TEETERS ON THE BRINK

	Italy	UK
Unemployment	11.6%	4.9%
Youth unemployment	36.5%	13.7%
Growth since 2008	-8.7%	+7%
Growth forecast 2016	0.9%	1.7%
Growth forecast 2017	1%	1.3%
Public debt (% of GDP)	135%	87%

Monte dei Paschi di Siena Share price
€2.0 1.5 1.0 0.5

and so flowing for the banking system, and then out to the markets—starts to become much more shaky. And I think that's what we're going to have by the end of this year, because now we're sort of in this period of the Fed raising rates, and other central banks have not. Mexico has. Some countries have done it in tandem, because they want to keep their currencies somewhat in an unofficial band relative to the dollar, but for the most part, it's still cheap money across the board.

But again, as it creeps up ever so little, everything becomes more expensive, everything becomes tighter, and that's when what has happened to the markets, and to the banking system, in terms of subsidies, starts to crumble. And I think we're kind of at that breaking point. It might be after another 25 basis points, maybe another 50 basis points, if the Fed goes there—but we're at a point where debt just starts to become very expensive, and then falls start to come in.

Gallagher: And you've been talking this week to a number of people on the Hill about Glass-Steagall. What's the importance of the role of Glass-Steagall? Is it in preventing this threatening situation, or do you think it's just a question of whether we need it in order to get the banks in order, in order for them to do sound banking?

Prins: Well, I think it's both. First of all, when we had Glass-Steagall repealed in 1999, it unleashed a tremendous amount of mergers throughout the banking industry. So we already have big banks dominating a lot of the trading, and a lot of issuance, and a lot of deposit holding anyway, because we've had the 1994 act where they could go across state lines, and we had a 1999 act of repealing Glass-Steagall, so they could now connect to insurance companies, asset management firms and investment banking, all within one roof, connected to commercial banking and deposits and loans.

So as that was all happening, banks were consolidating; they were becoming either bigger—if they were sort of a supermarket commercial bank, like a JPMorgan Chase, or Citigroup where they chose to merge a sort of classic commercial banking company with an investment banking company—or else they became more leveraged, like what happened with Goldman Sachs and Morgan Stanley. Because Goldman and Morgan Stanley didn't merge with a bank and have that extra balance sheet, those extra deposits from which to leverage new securities, or trade, or bets, to create more risky opportunities for themselves in the market, they chose to compete against these supermarket banks that were created in the wake of Glass-Steagall repeal, by leveraging themselves even more. That's what Lehman Brothers did before it imploded; that's what Bear Stearns—which I used to work at before they imploded. So there was a sort of competition in leverage that was unleashed by Glass-Steagall being repealed.

What that created was this hunt, as it turned out in this period, for subprime loans, which could be leveraged into securities, and they could be merged into new securities and CDOs (collateralized debt obligations), where there were all sorts of layers on top of these individual loans, but all of those layers were leveraged within a security. And then the banks themselves were borrowing more and more to buy, or create, more of these securities, so they were leveraging their balance sheets even more.

So you had leverage on the balance sheets, and leverage on the security.

Gallagher: Just so people understand, who aren't familiar with the language: By leverage, you mean putting a lot more debt on their balance sheets, to make their assets seem more profitable.

Prins: Yes, for book leverage. You're putting more debt—you're basically borrowing money in order to create securities, and that could be by borrowing money to buy more loans, in order to create securities out of them and then resell them. It could be borrowing money to get more involved in the derivatives markets. It could be a lot of different things, but you're effectively—it's like if you were to go to, say, Vegas, and bet on a table. You can either do it with your ten dollars, or your hundred dollars in your pocket, or you can use your credit card—and you can sort of leverage up. It could be like I want an extra hundred, an extra hundred, and I'll go to the machine and then you keep on sort of doubling, tripling, quadrupling, and 20 times down on one bet. So you lose 20 to 1 instead of one to one, if it goes against you. And that's basically what happened in the markets, on the back of these subprime loans.

The only reason that was allowed, that that was *able* to happen, was because of the structure of Wall Street, that enabled banks to take loans, both off their own books and to buy them onto their books, and repackage them and resell them into more complex, more risky securities. If Glass-Steagall had existed, they would not have been able to do that. If Glass-Steagall had existed, banks would not have borrowed and been allowed to leverage as much in competition with the banks that had the loans to begin with, in order to do that. So the repeal of Glass-Steagall allowed the crisis to happen, because it allowed this instability in the banking system; it allowed banks to become bigger; it allowed them to become too big to fail after they began to implode—and the Treasury Department, the Federal Reserve, and the government decided, we need to basically save the economy, save citizens, from the implosion of these banks.

And so we're going to plug the holes. We're going to plug the holes with TARP, we're going to plug the holes with bailouts, we're going to plug the holes with lending more to these banks, because they can't even get any money, because they sort of shot what they've had into these bets, into the market, and that's not working right now. We'll give them zero interest rates, so that money can come more cheaply back to them. All of these remedies they just talked about a little bit before,

were really created to subsidize a very flawed system from a structural perspective.

And so now we have this flawed system that never got readjusted back to something that would be more stable for everybody. But now it's elevated by all this extra subsidy, and extra debt, that was thrown in, to keep it from completely dying in 2007-2008. So that's why the risk of implosion right now, the downside is much greater, because we never really bothered to dissect these deposits and these loans from all the securities that were created, and can still be created, and the leverage that can still be created upon them.

So now it's almost more imperative to reinstate Glass-Steagall, to bring back that separation, because we're actually on the hock for more money. The books, for example, of the Federal Reserve are now four and a half or so trillion dollars, and they've increased their reserves from these banks, including with excess reserves the banks don't even have to put there, of something like two trillion or so dollars. That's two trillion dollars that's off the top of our economy, that effectively was created in debt by the Treasury Department, went through the primary dealers, these biggest conglomerate banks, and was sold back, basically given back to the Fed to receive interest from the Fed.

So there's a sort of triangle of debt and money moving around doing absolutely nothing—that's something like two trillion, and that's only the United States. There's mortgages and other things on the Fed books. The same thing has happened in Europe, the same has happened in Japan—there's been this circle of debt creation by governments to go through the biggest banks, and go back to their central banks without ever going into the economy. And that shows you the problem. The reason these big banks need to be split up, is so that they don't have to have emergency money in excess reserves at these central banks, in case their risky bets go south again—which is why they have it there, why they're not necessarily putting the rest of that into the individuals' or citizens' part of the economy.

They would have to do that if they were split up, as they were under Glass-Steagall, into banks that just dealt with deposits and loans, and banks that could trade all they wanted to, and buy and sell all the risky securities they wanted to, but on their own dime, and not be bailed out by the government if they fail.

Italian Finance Committee To Hold Hearings on Banking Separation

by Claudio Celani

March 17—On March 15, the Finance Committee of the Italian Chamber of Deputies began to examine and discuss various proposals for banking separation, in what one committee member described as "an historic moment." Indeed, literally dozens of draft bills for re-establishing strict separation between commercial and investment banks, all of them referring to Franklin Roosevelt's 1933 Glass-Steagall Act, have been introduced in past and current sessions in both the Chamber and the Senate—but only now has the decision been taken to schedule a discussion and a vote, first in the Committee and eventually on the floor.

The importance of this debate has been understood internationally. U.S. Representative Walter Jones (R-NC), himself a co-initiator of the new Glass-Steagall bill in the U.S. Congress, sent a message to Finance Committee chairman Maurizio Bernardo, and to committee member Alessio Villarosa who filed the most recent among the twelve draft bills now being examined in Rome.

In his message, Rep. Jones commended the Italian Parliament "for their leadership in bringing forward the debate on the need for reinstatement of Glass-Steagall legislation. As a Republican in the United States Congress, I have joined with [Democratic] Congresswoman Marcy Kaptur (Ohio) in introducing legislation, HR 790, for the reinstatement of Glass-Steagall. It is my

LaRouche PAC

hope that the United States Congress will follow the Italian leadership and bring a debate to the United States House of Representatives, because I believe this to be in the best interest of the American people."

The movement towards Glass-Steagall in Italy is a direct or indirect result of the years-long campaign by the LaRouche movement, whose milestone was the first draft bill introduced by Senator Oskar Peterlini in 2012. At least four of the current twelve draft bills in the lower Chamber have been directly influenced, or even co-drafted, by the LaRouche movement.

LPAC-TV

creative commons

Rep. Walter Jones   *Rep. Marcy Kaptur*

proceeding, and proposed to adopt a "basic text" before going to hearings.

Committee chairman Maurizio Bernardo said that even a basic text could not be adopted before going deeper into the issue, and that hearings would aim at that. With that, the discussion was adjourned to a future date. The next step will be the hearing, and much depends on the authority and the effectiveness of the "experts" called in by the government and by the opposition. Our readers are encouraged to send messages to the Committee Chairman and to the Rapporteur, in order to make them feel the pressure:

Maurizio Bernardo (chairman):
bernardo_m@camera.it
Marco di Maio (rapporteur):
dimaio_marco@camera.it
Alessio Villarosa (Author, Draft Bill C 4255):
villarosa_a@camera.it

Unfortunately, the government is notoriously submissive to the European Union regime, i.e. opposed to Glass-Steagall. However, it did not dare to take any position in the first meeting, which is a sign of insecurity.

Rapporteur Marco Di Maio (of the Democratic Party, which leads the current government), presented the texts of the bills, and at the same time those of various fake "reforms" introduced in the U.S.A., in the UK and in the EU—while endorsing none of them. In an effort to show an appearance of objectivity, the government proposed to hold hearings in order to clarify the issue.

In the ensuing discussion, Committee members demanded that the government clearly state its position, whether in favor or opposed to Glass-Steagall. Deputy Alessio Villarosa (M5S) stressed that the present discussion is of historic value, as for the first time an issue is being addressed which the country has expected for years. Villarosa said he is in favor of hearings, but that it is fundamental to know whether the rapporteur (the government) is prejudiced against banking separation, or whether the government was willing to have an open discussion. Di Maio replied that his proposal to hold hearings is already evidence of willingness by the government to discuss the issue. Its definitive position will depend on the results of the investigation.

Pietro Laffranco (Forza Italia) said he was in favor of strict separation, as he had cosigned one of the draft bills, and he too requested a clear position from the majority before organizing hearings that could be a waste of time.

Davide Zoggia (MDP) also demanded clarity before

REVIVE GLASS-STEAGALL NOW!

LaRouchePAC is now leading a nationwide effort to push through legislation for Glass-Steagall
(www.larouchepac.com).

"The point is, we need Glass-Steagall immediately. We need it because that's our only insurance to save the nation.... Get Glass-Steagall in, and we can work our way to solve the other things that need to be cleaned up. If we don't get Glass-Steagall in first, we're in a mess!"
—*Lyndon LaRouche, Feb. 11, 2013*

WATCH the LaRouchePAC video:
'Glass-Steagall: Signing a Revolution'

SUBSCRIBE to EIR Online
www.larouchepub.com/eiw
toll-free: **1-800-278-3135**
e-mail: fulfullment@larouchepub.com

Obama's War Crimes in Yemen Saved Al-Qaeda

by Ulf Sandmark, *EIR* correspondent, Stockholm

March 15—The Yemen war is one of the worst of Obama's crimes. Millions of Yemenis, the majority of the population, have been blocked from food deliveries for two years by Obama and the Saudis, causing the biggest current starvation crisis in the world. Fourteen million Yemenis are starving, according to the UN, and children are dying at an accelerated pace, as *EIR* reported on Mar. 3 of this year.

Just as Al-Qaeda in the Arabian Peninsula (AQAP) and ISIS were about to be wiped out of Yemen by the regular army with its allied Houthi forces almost exactly two years ago, on March 26,

Xinhua Photo

People search for victims inside a funeral hall after it was targeted by airstrikes in Sana'a, Yemen, on Oct. 8, 2016.

2015, the nation was attacked by a Saudi-led alliance in what has become a genocidal bombing campaign and war on Yemen. Obama joined the military aggression of the Saudi-led coalition, supplying intelligence, target lists and refueling for bomber jets. Saudi Arabia and its allies brought together troops and mercenaries from different parts of the world. What was not mentioned in Western media were the open statements by Al-Qaeda leaders pledging to join the Saudis in attacking the new Yemeni political leadership and especially the Houthi movement (Ansarullah). Al-Qaeda became part of the foot soldiers of the Saudi-led alliance, and was never attacked by the Saudi air force. It restored its presence in Yemen with the help of the war.

On Oct. 27, 2015, the spokesman for the Syrian Arab Army reported that "four planes arrived in Aden Airport in Yemen, Oct. 16, carrying terrorists from ISIS. The spokesman said that the planes, which consisted of two Turkish Airlines planes, one Qatar Airways plane, and one Emirates Airlines plane, were carrying more than 500 ISIS members who had fled Syria following the Russian airstrikes." He went on to say that "upon arrival in Aden, the Saudi alliance officers divided them into three groups ... to join the alliance's forces which had sustained great losses during their battles there."[1] Even though this report was a single shot without confirmation elsewhere, the fact is that not only AQAP, but also ISIS terrorists gained influence in Yemen at the time.

Without mentioning any airlift from Turkey, Re-

---

1. http://sana.sy/en/?p=59341

Sana'a, Yemen, Oct. 9, 2015, months after an airstrike destroyed more than 100 buildings.

uters reported on June 30, 2015, that ISIS was growing to rival AQAP in Yemen. The article straightforwardly admitted the role of the terrorists in the Saudi-led alliance: "AQAP still participates in almost daily battles with the [Shi'a] Houthis alongside tribal fighters, Southern Resistance forces and supporters of exiled President Abd-Rabbu Mansour al-Hadi."[2]

The U.S. forces deployed for the Yemen war have stayed far away from the ground forces of the Saudi-led coalition, but maintain a total overview of the brutal Saudi campaign, most notably through U.S. special forces deployed in the Saudi command center to provide intelligence and target lists for the brutal bombing campaign by the Saudi air force. The U.S. Air Force aided the Saudi airplanes with airborne refueling to considerably extend their bombing capabilities, and also supplied guided bombs and cluster bombs that have been used against Yemen. The Obama Administration was forced to cut back the number of U.S. troops aiding the Saudi targeting operations, when a funeral reception was hit in Sana'a on Oct. 8, 2016, killing more than 150 and wounding more than 600 people with a "double tap" bombing, a war crime targeting the first responders. The United States was also forced to halt the deliveries of guided bombs.

The British Neocolonial Suffocation of Yemen

The British, who control both Obama and the Saudi

2. http://www.reuters.com/article/us-yemen-security-islamicstate-insight-idUSKCN0PA1T920150630

monarchy, have themselves kept a lower profile and never officially joined the Saudi-led alliance. However, they post soldiers in the Saudi command center for "targeting assistance" to the Saudis to control the slaughter. Further, the Saudi air force would not be able to fly without the extensive ground services of the British arms supplier BAE. After the Yemenis achieved independence from the British colonial system in the course of the 1960s, the British have overseen six wars there to keep Yemen down. The main instrument of the British in doing that, has been the Saudis, who fear a strong Republican Yemen that would set an example for the all the dissidents within the Gulf monarchies.

Saudi influence in Yemen has sustained dissent and discord there. Saudi Arabia has kept contact with, and financed some of the most influential tribes in Yemen. The Saudis also funded the rise of the extremist variety of Saudi Islam, Wahhabism, in Yemen, which did not exist before in this nation, which has a very tolerant tradition of different religions and sects living side by side. Yemen therefore witnessed many internal conflicts. In 2004, the Houthi movement was in an armed conflict with the national army and the President Ali Abdullah Saleh, who was supported by the Saudis at the time.

After the "Arab Spring" began in 2011, President Saleh was forced to resign in 2012 and a general dialogue and reconciliation process started. Saudi Arabia and the Gulf Cooperation Council (GCC) kept meddling in this process with their "GCC Initiative" that was meant to keep the old structures and give more influence to tribal forces rather than a strong and centralized national government. In that prolonged process, no presidential elections were possible, and instead the Yemeni parliament was obliged in February 2012 to "appoint" Abd Rabbuh Mansur Hadi as acting president for a limited two-year period, which was renewed until February 2015. Continued corruption, political oppression of the youth of the revolution, and the expanding influence of AQAP and ISIS, forced some national forces to act.

National Alliance for the Salvation of Yemen

The main formerly warring forces in Yemen, the Houthi forces on the one hand, and on the other the regular army of Yemen, which is largely very much under the influence of former president Saleh and his party, the National People's Congress, started to reconcile and cooperate. In this process of national reorganization, appointed President Abd Rabbuh Mansur Hadi was put under house arrest on Jan. 20, 2015, just before his term was to expire. Instead of resigning when his term expired, Hadi fled on March 21 to the major harbor town and old center for British control, Aden. Although he had lost

President Barack Obama and Yemen's President, Abd Rabbuh Mansur Hadi talk to the media as they meet at the White House, August 1, 2013, in Washington.

power and the control over the ministries, the capital, and the majority of the population, he called for armed "resistance" against the Sana'a government. From his home town, he claimed he still was the president and denounced the takeover as illegitimate.

The national alliance of the Houthis and the regular army of Yemen pursued the very limited forces of Hadi. In this process, in cleaning out the Saudi control of Yemen, AQAP was also pushed back to very limited areas in southeast Yemen. Just as the national alliance was about to seize Aden, the Saudi-led alliance launched the current war on Yemen on March 26, 2015. Former president Hadi, in whose name the attack was done, was not even informed of the launching of the war until three days afterwards.

Pakistani scholar Sikander Ahmed Shah, in successfully advising his government not to join the war against Yemen, pointed to the fact that former president Hadi had lost control over its capital and its territory, when, from Aden, he called for the Saudi-led military intervention. Shah wrote on April 6, 2015, that "... an intervention would not violate the sovereignty of Yemen if the incumbent government consents to or invites external military intervention... However, such assistance can only be lawfully provided if the incumbent government requesting it exercises 'effective control' over its territory... Under international law, it no longer enjoys effective control if it loses control over the capital city and is in 'imminent danger of col-

lapse.' Yemen is in the midst of the latter, where the capital city and sizable chunks of territory are under the control of the rebels. Control enjoyed by Hadi is limited to Aden and that too is not far from collapse. Therefore, legally speaking, relying on the president's consent for military intervention is highly problematic."[3]

The Yemen war therefore is not, as portrayed by Western media, primarily a civil war, but an attack on a sovereign member nation of the UN. The Pakistanis refused to become proxies for the British in this war. Egypt, another nation with experience of fighting in British-instigated wars, refused to send soldiers, although nominally supporting the war as a member of the Saudi-led alliance. British puppet Obama, however, rushed into this new regime-change war, like the wars against Iraq, Libya, and Syria. In a not-merely-symbolic move indicating Obama's complete allegiance to the Anglo-Saudi Empire, then-Saudi ambassador to the United States Adel Al-Jubair announced the start of "Operation Storm of Resolve" on March 26 at a news conference in Washington.

The Obama administration was later instrumental in supporting the UN Security Council Resolution 2216 on Yemen, which is used as a basis for the Saudi-led military aggression. This resolution was passed on April 14, 2015, a full three weeks after the

---

3 http://www.dawn.com/news/1174185

bombing started, and without any mention of it. The resolution was proposed by Jordan, one of the members of the Saudi-led coalition, and it provides only for a one-sided mediation process by the GCC nations. A veto in the UN Security Council could have stopped Resolution 2216, but tragically, China voted with the Western powers and Russia abstained. The Russian position is clear from an article in Sputnik News of May 2, 2015 where the late Russian UN Representative Vitaly Churkin insisted "that the UN Security Council's previous resolution on Yemen, 2216, did not authorize airstrikes by the Saudi Arabia-led Coalition... It is clear from Resolution 2216 that it did not authorize the use of military force. Some colleagues were saying that the Saudi-led coalition is trying to make sure that Resolution 2216 is implemented. This is not the case. Their action is completely outside the resolution."[4]

Resolution 2216 further provides for an arms blockade, which has resulted in mission creep allowing for a full land, sea, and air blockade of food, medicine, and fuel, causing the genocide against the Yemeni people. The Obama Administration in this way allowed for both war crimes and the worst starvation crisis in the world. On top of that, the killer Obama continued his personally directed drone warfare ostensibly against AQAP in Yemen.[5]

The Backlash against the Drones

The drone warfare is creating a tremendous backlash of hate against the United States in Yemen and in most of the Arab street in the whole region. What in the Orwellian language of the Obama Administration was called "collateral damage" in these strikes, are pure and simple massacres of families, neighbors, or innocent bystanders. Rules of decision making in the White House Tuesday kill sessions specified that if more than the targeted person on Obama's "baseball card" risked being killed, then Obama personally always had to take the decision, i.e. for the massacres of families.

The drone attacks killing families and bystanders as "collateral damage" in Yemen are so generally hated in Yemen, that even those who are at war against AQAP and ISIS are protesting. The Yemenis point to the reck-

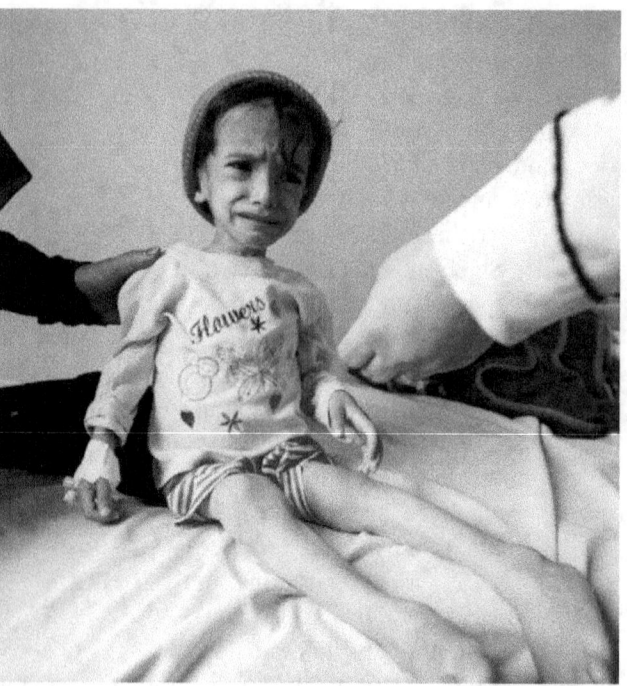

UNICEF/UNI191720/Yasin

A malnourished 2-year-old girl receiving treatment at a hospital in Sana'a.

less targeting, the absence of any justice, the devaluation of human life, the brutal infringement on their sovereignty and more. They also protest because Obama's drone war helped AQAP and ISIS in their recruitment, bringing still more drone attacks.

These protests continued under President Trump, too. The U.S. Navy Seal raid on Jan. 29 in a Yemeni village in the Al-Baidha province killed 70 people, among them 16 women and children. The picture of eight-year old Nora al-Awlaki, killed in the operation, with her red hair rosette, went viral in Yemen. As another drone hit a few days later, a demonstration against the drone war was organized in Sana'a March 3, where tens of thousands of armed men, who are themselves at war against the terrorists of Al-Qaeda and ISIS, poured out in anger into the streets.[6]

Anyone who has studied the history of war, knows that no war can be won by airstrikes alone, not even with complementary action by special forces. The terrorists in Yemen, just like those in Iraq and Syria, have to be defeated by the regular army and the blocking of supplies from foreign interests. What is needed beyond that, is the power of the nation mobilizing for recon-

4. https://sputniknews.com/amp/politics/20150502102162O895/
5. http://www.larouchepub.com/other/2017/4410obm_good_at_killing.html

6. https://www.youtube.com/watch?v=a15kKFiltZY

youtube/rt

Yemen: Mass demonstration in Sana'a decries Saudi-led coalition war.

struction and peaceful development, giving the youth a positive life alternative, instead of the terrorist death cults.

The Yemen Government

In the Yemeni capital of Sana'a, President Saleh Al-Samad is serving as the acting president pending the presidential election, as the Constitution of the Republic of Yemen requires. The National Salvation government was recognized on Dec. 10, 2016, in its latest formation by the Yemeni parliament majority elected before the war. The Houthi movement is but a part, although a very important part, of this broad national government.

This national coalition government is in administrative control of the ministries and public authorities, including the national army, as well as the majority of the population. The people of Yemen demonstrated its most determined and widest support of the acting president and his government in the exceptional demonstration in Sana'a of Aug. 20, 2016, in which two million Yemenis took part, despite ongoing bombardment. A new million-man demonstration is planned in Sana'a for the second anniversary of the beginning of the war on March 26. The government and its public authorities are the only ones capable of receiving and distributing the absolutely necessary foreign emergency aid,

because the harbor of Aden and its surroundings are under the control of militias and terrorists, making it too unsafe for the UN aid agencies to approach the shore. The government has a plan for taking part in the New Silk Road, and is therefore bringing hope for the reconstruction and future development of the nation.

Those who think that there is a way to get at Iran via Yemen, are wrong. Iran is playing no practical role in this war. The claim that the Houthis are proxies for Iran against Saudi Arabia, collapses under the fact that Yemen is under a total sea blockade. Most of the weapons, used in the war by the Sana'a government forces of the national army and Houthi tribesmen, were given to Yemen under the massive arms transfer, especially from the United States, for the fight against terrorism beginning in 2001. At the time the former president, Ali Abdullah Saleh, was an ally of the United States in the fake war against AQAP in Yemen. There are plenty of arms in Yemen, especially as the Saudis in the war also brought even more weapons that could be seized by the Sana'a government forces.

It is high time to end this genocidal war, which was made possible by the collusion of President Obama with the Anglo-Saudi Empire, and to bring about a completely new American and international policy vis-à-vis Yemen: Stop the war, start the reconstruction of the admittedly poorest country in the region, and integrate Yemen into the 21st Century's greatest peace project, China's "One Belt, One Road," the New Silk Road. With a positive collaboration between China, Russia and the United States, with the national forces and the youth of Yemen, this country could be made a "pearl in the necklace of the New Silk Road," as Helga Zepp-LaRouche pleaded in her statement to the International Schiller Institute conference in Berlin on June 26, 2016.

www.ingramcontent.com/pod-product-compliance
Lightning Source LLC
Chambersburg PA
CBHW080834310526
45788CB00020B/3556